DATE DUE

RESPONSIBILITY IN BUSINESS

Issues and Problems

BLAIR J. KOLASA

Dean of the School of Business Administration
Duquesne University

PRENTICE-HALL, INC.: ENGLEWOOD CLIFFS, N.J.

To My Family

Library of Congress
Catalog Card Number: 72-170645

ISBN: 0-13-773739-4

10 9 8 7 6 5 4 3 2 1

Prentice-Hall International, Inc., *London*
Prentice-Hall of Australia, Pty., Ltd., *Sydney*
Prentice-Hall of Canada, Ltd., *Toronto*
Prentice-Hall of India Private Limited, *New Delhi*
Prentice-Hall of Japan, Inc., *Tokyo*

CONTENTS

3

THE "NOW" ISSUES 23

PART 2
PROBLEMS: THE INDIVIDUAL
IN THE ORGANIZATION

4

INDIVIDUAL DEVELOPMENT 43

5

EQUALITY AND PRIVACY 53

6

ROLE REQUIREMENTS 65

PART 3
PROBLEMS: THE ORGANIZATION IN SOCIETY

7

RELATIONSHIPS WITH OTHER UNITS 77

8

RELATIONSHIPS WITH CONSUMERS 86

THE COMMUNITY 99

10

THE ENVIRONMENT 112

APPENDIX A 121

Public Law 88-352 — July 2, 1964
Civil Rights Act of 1964
Title VII — Equal Employment Opportunity

APPENDIX B 125

Public Law 90-321 — May 29, 1968
Consumer Credit Protection Act
Title I — Consumer Credit Cost Disclosure

APPENDIX C 128

Allegheny County Health Department
Rules and Regulations

APPENDIX D 133

Act No. 222, Session of 1970

APPENDIX E 137

Code of Professional Ethics

APPENDIX F 143

PREFACE

The growing awareness by businessmen of their responsibility beyond making a profit is characteristic of the present industrial and business scene. The importance of recognizing this responsibility and doing something about it is acknowledged, though often there may be an almost embarrassed discussion of the area. Abstract concepts of "justice" or "equality" may be raised, but the difficulty of applying the results of discussion to the solution of practical problems has been with us for a long time.

This short book represents a preference for coming to grips with problems that face decision-makers in organizations every day of their working lives. It tries to avoid platitudes or conceptualizations that may prevail in merely academic debates; instead, it places the reader in contexts that simulate real situations that call for problem-solving responses.

The text uses problems rather than case histories. The distillation from a larger and more complex set of facts focuses the attention of the reader upon the central aspects of the problem area rather than requiring him to wade through an excess of material that may not be directly related to the question at hand.

ACKNOWLEDGMENTS

The environment in which a written work develops has a great deal to do with the emergence of the final product. At Duquesne, superior officers provided administrative support while my colleagues were sympathetic in adjusting to the vagaries of time or other variables. The various clerical and typing tasks were cheerfully handled by Francis Carroll, Maryann Pilarski, and Donna Mills. Not least valuable, also, were the suggestions from a few of my students for seven of the selected problems. I owe thanks for these to Douglas High, Joseph Griffith, Edward J. Sullivan, Michael Roteman, Gil Stone, Peter Segall, E. A. Roskovensky, Edward M. Petrie, and Richard A. Casali.

Of my colleagues, Robert Broughton of the Duquesne Law School was especially helpful in providing materials and advice.

Those who were asked to review the present material have been most generous in their guidance in various stages of the project.

Dr. Joseph W. McGuire, Vice President, University of California

Dr. Joseph L. Massie, Acting Dean, University of Kentucky

Dr. Rick Pollay, University of British Columbia

At the same time they cannot be included in any critical comments directed at the final copy of the text.

If they are fortunate, authors receive extensive help from their publishers; so it has been in this instance. Chester Lucido, Daniel Kennedy, and many others in Prentice-Hall, Inc., have been most supportive in this effort and have helped to make the task an exciting one.

HOW TO USE THIS BOOK

The first three chapters provide an orientation to the area, with several concepts and issues related to social responsibility outlined in a few pages. Much more remains to be covered, of course, and the reader is encouraged to pursue those points that are of interest to him in works specifically designed to treat the concepts of social responsibility and ethics in depth. The present material should provide enough information and ideas, however, for a discussion of ramifications of each of the problems presented later.

The problems provide a basis for the learning process. Analysis of the situation presented, along with the questions that follow, should lead to the development of an understanding of the multiple ramifications of simple events. It is important to do this within a framework of logical procedures, using empirical evidence and avoiding the speculation so commonly associated with dormitory "bull sessions." It is vital, too, that the reader retain an openness to other alternatives that could be present in the problem-solving framework; the questions posed with the problems are only a sample of the number of questions that might be raised.

The instructor serves as a guide through the many pathways, some of them not clearly charted, that can be followed. Here a professor does not teach; he helps to provide the conditions for effective student learning. In utilizing Socratic techniques, the discussion leader may raise other alternatives available by asking the student to consider the further consequences of any problem-solving action.

The serious student is urged to consult, in addition, the material in the appendix.

PART 1

CONCEPTS AND ISSUES

1

THE NATURE OF
SOCIAL RESPONSIBILITY

No one has to tell the businessman of today that his job consists of more than simply working toward a profit. On all sides there are signs and portents that signal the broader and more socially significant message that the deeper internal and wider environmental factors in business and society require attention. Personnel policies that do not take into account their impact upon individual freedom and development are not likely to keep the organization or the insensitive administrator in a healthy economic state for long. In the same way, a disregard of the changing cultural or sociopolitical conditions surrounding the business entity can be the basis for much consternation, or worse, in the ranks of those managers who may have learned their lessons in accounting and finance well but who either do not or cannot comprehend the wider social base of their fiscal or technical activities.

A concern for the impact of economic power upon other persons, both on an individual basis and in the aggregate, marks a clearly developing trend in today's business. It may be inaccurate to say that this feeling is enthusiastically accepted or even widely recognized by businessmen, yet the trend to social responsibility is strong. Such concerns permeate every fact situation with which the decision-maker in business is faced. The many and varied problems that appear later in this text could be labeled with the traditional designations — personnel problems, principles of management, the environment of business, or many others. All contain the elements of social concern, ethics, morals, or responsibility that come into play in technical or professional decisions. The centrality of social responsibility is clear even when the focus may be on other substantive elements.

There are varied opinions identifying the bases for this newer posture of businessmen. A simplistic view might ascribe the change to the development of insight or to more acute feelings with regard to ethical conduct, possibly resulting from a higher general level of education. Others see the entire process as further illustration of the lessening of managerial control over all phases of the enterprise as outside forces or nonmanagerial groups internally take over the direction of activities. These points of view can be rejected in favor of a more functional position that regards the newer attitudes as rational responses by administrators and organizations to the changes in the sociopolitical surroundings. According to this view, the actions of business decision-makers may be seen to generate changes in the sociopolitical environment, or, at the very least, to reflect changes in that environment. There are strong indications, however, that there is an influence process in both directions; businessmen do have an impact upon the environment even though there may be stronger forces from the outside acting upon the decision-makers in business organizations.

Many of today's executives have recognized the newer roles they must play in the changing environment. Enough have embraced these new postures for the situation to have reached the point where, as Cheit (1964, p. 152) puts it, they are preaching the "Gospel of Social Responsibility." (For those who prefer the use of business terminology, the activists may be said to be "selling" social responsibility.) Generally, however, the campaign is sober, subdued, and much less ideological than the almost revivalistic preaching that often accompanied the earlier positions of "saving free enterprise." This almost silent campaign remains an important factor in the business world despite the increasingly vociferous attempts on the part of some groups to undermine public confidence in the commitment of businessmen to social responsibility. Even individuals who have not been content to present their views in a rational and verbal way, but have translated their positions into violent acts, have been met with restrained responses on the part of business representatives. This posture by businessmen may reflect the rational kinds of decision-making derived from and influenced by their education for business. On the other hand, there are some observers who see the reactions as emanating from a basic self-consciousness that comes from being thrust into an unfamiliar role. The notion of social responsibility, or even an extensive awareness of the basic social factors surrounding corporate existence, may indeed be lacking in the corporate picture.

The drive toward social responsibility in its present form and extent is a relatively recent topic in the discussion of the role of business, although it has deep roots in history. Certainly ancient Greek views of commerce and the teachings of Saint Thomas Aquinas may be said to have served as a few, among many, of the attitudinal antecedents of today's postures. More recently, the critics of industrial practices in the United States at the turn of the century undoubtedly mustered some sympathy and support, or at least thoughtful consideration, in the ranks of the companies they scrutinized. The development of the Progressive Party in the national political arena was due in great part to an ideology that incorporated concepts of concern about the aftermaths of business decisions. The decade of the 1950s witnessed the emergence of the feelings of social responsibility in many written and spoken statements, well represented by *Management Creeds and Philosophies: Top Management Guides in Our Changing Economy* (Thompson, 1958), a document commissioned by the American Management Association. In the 1960s social unrest and discord were met with increasing response from industry spokesmen, both in the way of public relations campaigns or in the form of specific action-oriented programs. Eastman Kodak, U.S. Steel, and the Ford Motor Co. have been involved in various ways in alleviation of variances in employment policies, particularly along racial lines. Other companies, like Dow Chemical and Gulf Oil, have borne the brunt of the dissatisfaction with American foreign policy, expressed in boycotts and demonstrations against the company, its personnel, and products. The 1970s will bear witness to the already widespread concern with ecology and the problems involved in pollution of the environment by industry. Virtually every business entity has already been faced with its share of this problem.

What is Social Responsibility?

A complex concept can have as many meanings as there are individuals who attempt to employ it; so it is with social responsibility. Common usage however, provides a consensus sufficient for forming a base for discussion. The dictionary (Funk & Wagnalls) defines *responsibility* as:

> (1) the state of being responsible, answerable, or accountable.
> (2) *Ethics*. The status of personality considered as capable of responding to the obligations established by moral law or by ethical principles and ideals, however derived.

Both of these definitions are important to the manager and, even though the focus of this book may be on the second, the accountability of the decision-maker is always in evidence in the results of decisions. Thus these two aspects of responsibility are inseparable. In both there is some further question as to whether the term *social* even needs to be added, since responsibility implies a concern for others.

The concern for responding to what is "right" and in a way that "should be" is certainly not new, although there are always some elements of novelty in its various manifestations. Certain labels may have been more in evidence at various times, but it is clear that the discussions have generally been on the same topic. Even though the field has been delineated in terms of business ethics, morality, values, or — especially now — social responsibility, these terms have been used interchangeably to refer to the general feelings and behavior called for in the promotion of the common good. There may be some profit, however, in sketching the technical differences between terms.

The Elements

The discipline of ethics is primarily the handiwork of philosophers who usually restrict the use of the term. They point to a logical comparison that relates means to ends in an interconnected system constructed by use of reason or by rational methods.

The statement that "ethics is a science of judging specifically human ends and the relationship of means to those ends" (Garrett, 1966, p. 4) emphasizes the cognitive aspects of the situation, although many add, as Garrett himself does, an action orientation to this purely intellectual one by considering the issue of controlling those means so that they do indeed serve human ends. The two aspects can be referred to as the science of ethics on the one hand and as an art on the other. Business ethics should be considered as encompassing both aspects — the judgment of relationships and the use of techniques to serve those relationships. Indeed, of all human activities business can plausibly be seen as being among the most "practical," for the service of the firm in furthering human ends is immediate and specific. The impact of business decisions upon individuals and society makes the area of business prime territory for a consideration of ethics.

The view that ethics is more than just an intellectual exercise receives support from Walton (1969, p. 35), who interprets ethics as an applied discipline — "a practical science designed to test logically the rightness or wrongness of human acts." This position places emphasis upon the concept of the "reasonable man" — that is, a man whose reasonableness will lead him to act rightly within certain broadly defined limits, although it is not to be assumed that he will invariably do the right thing.

When the term *ethics* refers to a delimited philosophical view of means-end relationships as sketched above, it does not include the influence of the surrounding culture or theological orientations. The norms of society are understood to be important in determining behavior but the study of ethics sets out to evaluate these guidelines through the use of methods involving more ultimate tests of reason. Neither the cultural rules of a society nor the teachings of a religious group are to be considered in the determination of ethical conclusions, so that, theoretically, ethics is above these temporal influences; in reality, however, one may well question how little or how much the excluded factors influence the end result of philosophical inquiry. Certainly general behavior patterns result from an intertwining of all variables, so much so that the term *ethics* in common usage more often refers to the entire area, rather than only to the area of philosophical inquiry.

Morality is the set of attitudes or values shaped by the cultural setting in which behavior takes place. Since society plays an important role in forming personality, the influence process transcends the immediate feelings of the individual and what is right does not depend upon a personal whim at a particular moment. "Moral behavior is that which is governed by beliefs or feelings of what is right or wrong regardless of self-interest or immediate consequences of a decision to do or not to do specific things under particular conditions" (Barnard, 1958, p. 4). Various forces in society play their part in shaping those beliefs and feelings.

In contrast to ethical formulations, which are developed in philosophical activity, notions of morality are learned. In the process of individual development of attitudes and values, the family is the usual channel of transmission from the larger society even though other groupings or individuals can and do play a role. The incorporation by the individual of these determinants of behavior has been called *socialization*. In becoming socialized the person learns the social rules, or norms, of the group and comes to adopt supporting attitudes and predispositions to respond in certain ways to important personal and social issues.

Later individual decision-making, whether alone or in organized groups, is determined by these norms of society and the attitudes and values of those who function within the guidelines. When people ask, "Is this right, or good, or proper?" they are speaking in terms of the rightness, goodness, and propriety of an action as judged within the social framework in which the decision-makers have operated.

The contributions to morality that are made by religious ideologies may seem rather straightforward. Certainly there are precepts that are shared by all the world's great religions despite differences in their views of the roles of individuals or groups. But it is not enough to focus upon the "golden rule" or "love of one's fellow man" or any other approach that fails to go beyond obvious surface views. "Moral ideals, when expressed in general terms rather than in action in concrete situations, are necessarily abstract, and attainment may fall short of this abstract ideal. This does not mean failure is evidence of immorality, but that moral achievement is in part dependent on concrete conditions which vary widely" (Barnard, 1958, p. 4). Such "moral ideals" can be derived from empirical studies; a recent example (Senger, 1970) of this approach demonstrated that managers who were more religious than their colleagues were more socially responsible or humanistic in orientation and less economic in motivation. While the religious manager was more likely to be rated high by superiors, there was some evidence that his more traditional stance made him less open to newer and perhaps more effective responses. The outcome of this orientation may result in the pursuit of socially relevant goals by the company but, importantly, the religious manager would be likely to proceed along the paths followed in the past — increased employment, improved working conditions, and contributions to familiar charities. His efforts, then, might be less than optimally effective because he is meeting new and complex problems with traditional solutions.

The lesson to be learned may be that good intentions, as always, are not enough.

ELEMENTS OF THE ETHOS
(Adapted from Walton, 1969, p. 24)

Area	Religious	Philosophic	Cultural
Source	Diety	Man	Society
Method	Faith	Logic	Experience
Body of Knowledge	Moral Theology	Ethics	Social Norms

THE BASIC VALUE CONTINUUM

(THE ETHOS)

In one attempt at an integration of the preceding concepts, Walton (1969, p. 24) refers to this area as the *ethos,* which is conceived of as a value continuum comprising the "all embracing field within which different types of values (religious, ethical, socio-economic, and cultural) are found." The *ethos* is more than ethics or morals in that it accommodates more values than are considered in purely philosophical or social evaluations. Because of its comprehensive nature, this value continuum can serve as the basis for social responsibility.

The contributions to the field of others from religion, society, and the philosophers are clear but there still remains the problem of arranging them to firm up the framework of social responsibility. A broad statement that identifies socially responsible activity as that undertaken for the "common good" or "in the public interest" will receive general support even if it provides little information. Better understanding comes with a perusal of specific viewpoints.

Though he recognizes that such simple statements will not solve problems, Garrett (1966, p. 7) emphasizes the role of the individual by going beyond the mere statement that responsibility is something that promotes a good. This "good" can be accomplished through "whatever truly promotes the growth of the individual and the means available to him." In any setting of priorities the group must yield to concern for the individual, for "the person is not a means to the perfection of society, the state or anything else. . . . Societies are means to the real perfection of the individual."

Emphasis can be placed upon decision-making and the resulting consequences, so that the socially responsible businessman is one "who realizes that his decisions may have consequences outside his firm and that he will try to make these private decisions so that the consequences accord with generally accepted values" (Cheit, 1964, p. 160). But interactions within the firm must be considered as well. All actions are governed by a set of attitudes and values that operate on a normative basis. Whether a decision involves the health, safety, or welfare of a larger number of individuals in an outside aggregate, or whether only one person within an organization is affected makes no basic difference. What touches one man concerns all of mankind. The treatment of a worker by a foreman, of a student by a teacher, or of a citizen by a government official reflects and affects that society.

The impact of the business corporation upon society is further highlighted in a description of social responsibility (Walton, 1967, p. 18) that emphasizes the "intimacy of the relationships between the corporation and society and realizes that such relationships must be kept in mind by top managers as the corporation and the related groups pursue their respective goals." By recognizing that the action of the corporation is voluntary in connection with other voluntary organizations, one recognizes also that the corporation is not forced to do whatever it may do. Further, the corporation must recognize that all its activity may not be measurable in the same terms as are used in gauging the economic returns in the primary effort of the enterprise.

These verbal definitions are still not enough for our purposes, however. Results come primarily through the translating of verbal constructs into actual behavior in real events. No matter how much men may agree on the necessity for action in the community interest or for the good of the greatest number, there is always the problem of determining how this agreement may be realized in specific problem situations. Who decides what actions are to be taken or, more basically, whether the actions are in the public interest? It has been suggested by some cynics that business responsibility is defined by business and that socially responsible acts are those businessmen say are responsible. Of course, there is the danger that this will be the case, but it is a condition that is readily brought under control with an alert populace exposed to open channels of communications. Dissent, which may represent a variation of this political awareness, has been one of the characteristics of the American social scene. In addition, higher levels of education, leisure, and concern for others may be increasing the use of this and other monitoring tactics. Actions of organizations are being scrutinized more carefully and with increasing frequency by private individuals and groups.

In a complementary view, Walton (1967) emphasizes the need for businessmen to balance competing interests of various constituencies and to work closely with government in taking into account the rights of all involved, while rejecting, though in a restrained and reasonable way, those demands that are unjustified. This "balancing of interests" is an equilibrium model that derives from the concept of checks and balances grafted into the American federal system of government, or from the more basic social concept of pluralism, which sees the rights of groups as being served through competitive striving for control of their conditions of existence. This concept assumes that the competition assures some equity for all the strivers in society, inasmuch as each group has an opportunity to argue its case. Some may argue in more active and direct ways, however, while others may be handicapped by virtue of their lowly socioeconomic or political position, and will therefore be less able to compete for the attention of social policy-makers or decision-makers.

Counter Concerns

There are, of course, other views of the role of business in society. The strong thrust toward social responsibility is by no means a crusade, and strong dissenters from the prevailing position exist, some of whom are highly vocal. Most references to business operations emphasize the primary responsibility of the corporation to the stockholder, claiming that managers have "the single task of employing capital of their stockholder in the most profitable manner" rather than in any broader interest (Hayek, 1960). Levitt's (1958) thesis is similar and more positive. Welfare, says he, is the government's job — that of business is making money. The role of all major groups is to compete by pursuing their own paths so that no one entity dominates the society. Still other critics of the socially responsible viewpoint take a legalistic position and state that managers may not dispense the corporation's money in a manner extraneous to the direct efforts of the enterprise; the officers of the company are operating under a trust for the benefit of the stockholders.

These same feelings are not limited to business organizations; similar statements appear from activists in or observers of the labor scene. Many labor leaders feel they are acting in a socially responsible fashion when they fight to further the economic interests of the workers they represent. Any other approach "violates the ethics of . . . a trade union leader . . . no matter how worthy the purpose" (Brooks, 1963, p. 27). In much the same way, these advocates in all quarters equate the making of money for their constituents with social responsibility. Their position may be something of a variation of the old adage "build a better mousetrap and the world will beat a path to your door." According to this philosophy, the benefits accruing to one's interest group are the most appropriate index of social responsibility.

These criticisms have had responses, too. The legal argument has been answered by reminding its partisans that managers have long been justified in acting in ways that developed the good will of customers or of the community (Katz, 1960). McGuire (1965), among others, argues further that when costs are considered in a broad sense, the socially conscious corporation does not have higher unit costs, for employees may accept lower wages and customers may pay higher prices when a company has the reputation of being fair and active in promoting the welfare of the entire community.

The important conclusion may be that the community-minded corporation profits over the long term when it is not concerned with profit alone.

SUMMARY

Concern with social responsibility is becoming increasingly characteristic of business and industry as questions of this nature permeate all phases of organizational activity. Businessmen have had to learn to respond to new outside demands for greater and more direct action to solve a variety of social and environmental problems.

The precepts governing desirable social action are built up through the academic logic of ethics as well as through the norms of cultural and ideological groups. These center on the making of socially responsible decisions – those promoting the "public interest" or in the "common good." While general agreement may be reached on the verbal definition of responsibility (in reality people use the terms *ethics, morality,* and *responsibility* interchangeably), the important and more difficult task is the translation of the constructs into real situations.

The introduction of social responsibility in business is criticized by some who believe that this matter should be kept apart from the primary responsibility to the stockholders of the corporation. Some labor leaders even feel that an organization does its bit for society when it promotes the welfare of its members. These limited views may be categorized as examples of defining terms in too restrictive a manner.

BIBLIOGRAPHY

Barnard, C. (1958) Elementary Conditions of Business Morals. *California Management Review.* 1, 1–13.

Brooks, G. (1963) Ethical Responsibilities of Labor. *Stanford Business Bulletin,* p. 27.

Cheit, E. (1964) The New Place of Business: Why Managers Cultivate Social Responsibility. In E. Cheit, ed., *The Business Establishment.* New York: John Wiley & Sons.

Garrett, T. (1966) *Business Ethics.* New York: Appleton-Century-Crofts.

Hayek, F. (1960) The Corporation in a Democratic Society. In M. Anshem and G. Bach, eds., *Management and Corporations, 1985.* New York: McGraw-Hill.

Katz, W. (1960) Responsibility and the Modern Corporation. *Journal of Law and Economy,* 3, 75–85.

Levitt, T. (1958) The Dangers of Social Responsibility. *Harvard Business Review,* 36 (5), 41–50.

McGuire, J. (1965) The Social Responsibilities of the Corporation. In E. Flippo, ed., *Evolving Concepts in Management: Proceedings of the 24th Annual Meeting.* University Park, Pa.: Academy of Management.

Senger, J. (1970) The Religious Manager. *Academy of Management Journal,* 13 (2), 179–86.

Thompson, S. (1958) *Management Creeds and Philosophies: Top Management Guides in our Changing Economy.* New York: American Management Association.

Walton, C. (1967) *Corporate Social Responsibilities.* Belmont, California: Wadsworth Publishing Co.

_____ (1969) *Ethos and the Executive.* Englewood Cliffs, N. J.: Prentice-Hall, Inc.

2

WHY WE ARE WHERE WE ARE

Comments back and forth across the "generation gap" (if there is such a thing) are sometimes lively but not too varied. Oldsters often complain that the younger generation never "reads the minutes of the previous meetings" and therefore sets about to "reinvent the wheel" anew each time. Those who are newer to this planet sometimes answer that their fathers have made a mess of things anyway, so why bother finding out what has been done? As with most issues, both views have their valid points. It is inefficient to start from scratch time and again, but it is also dangerous to believe that what has worked before will work again, and even more dangerous to believe that what hasn't worked before will work now. A good decision-maker must have as many inputs in as short a time as possible, but his actions must be effective in solving problems. New situations indeed may call for approaches never used before.

What is of value in history is the possibility of a better understanding of the present state of an individual, organization, or nation; no knowledge of a person or a group is complete without knowing how they "got that way." The values supported by a society (the "right and proper" way to approach life events) have deep roots in the experiences of previous generations and the social heritage of today's peoples represents attitudes and beliefs that have been developed and passed on by those who have gone before.

Behavioral Themes

Our look back into history reveals the emergence of certain basic and powerful themes underlying human events and the attempts to explain them. These ideas are still very much alive and they persist in influencing the course of present-day events.

Among the most outstanding of these themes has been the opposition of the concern for individual rights on one hand and the desire to promote the strength of the group on the other. The demands of individualism and collectivism frequently have been irreconcilable as the result of the taking of extreme positions. Often, too, it has been difficult to identify the precise characteristics of ideological movements; even anarchic movements that have been proclaimed as efforts to free individuals sometimes have an authoritarian stamp. Present generations need not be limited to an abstract comparison of the historical teachings of this matter; the fundamental thrusts of these competing points of view may be identified in every controversy that ends up in the nation's highest court. Individual rights versus the concern for the group is a basic feature of each case.

Other broad views range from the Marxian notion of a synthesis of competing ideologies to a more restricted analysis of causes of social and economic change. One of the more interesting of the latter approaches is the tracing of relationships between a religious ideology and economic events. Thus an "ethic," or ideological life style, associated with some variants of Protestantism has been linked with the rise of capitalism in western Europe.

On an individual level there have been efforts to explain behavior through theories of motivation. Stating the problem in terms such as "men act in their own self-interest" may be an important first principle, but in itself it says very little. It is merely a familiar way of stating the basic factor of motivation and the economic and psychological mechanisms that may be active in the goal-directed satisfaction of needs. Power is a recurrent theme used to explain why men and nations act in certain ways. On another tack, hedonistic views state that men act to maximize their pleasure and to minimize their pain. Such views may show extensive variation, in that there may be many ways in which actions serve this basic purpose. Notions of social control through strict legal sanctions (pain) develop more readily in some circumstances than in others. A more positive approach focuses upon the effectiveness of reinforcing desirable behavior through rewards (pleasure).

Attempts to discover fundamental bases for behavior have sometimes led to the proclamation of a physical, innate, or "natural" course of events. The view that all human societies are competitive is one of these positions that continues to be widely held despite much anthropological evidence of cooperative or mixed situations. In the same way, many viewers of the social scene seized upon Darwin's evolutionary patterns and adapted them to social behavior. The doctrine of "survival of the fittest" can do double duty — in social behavior as well as in the physical way that Darwin outlined.

Questions pertaining to the influence of heredity or environment upon human behavior leave their mark too. Everyday decisions about hiring, promoting, or supporting social welfare programs may hinge upon the notions held about whether individuals can develop as the result of experience or are limited by their biological status. Can one "make silk purses out of sows ears" is no longer asked, but similar questions are.

Even legal constructs are of import here. The basic concept of *contract*, for instance, emphasizes the idea of an individual as responsible for his actions. "You made your bed — lie in it," is a position that underscores the bargaining entered into with others and the necessity for accepting the consequences. An alternate view holds that *status* is the concept to be considered; one's status, or position, in the society (dependent child, mother, handicapped person), rather than what has been bargained for, is the determining factor in social and economic relationships. It should be readily apparent to any prospective decision-maker, not just one in a business setting, that his reactions to social welfare programs, for instance, can be influenced by a predisposition on this level of which he may be essentially unaware but which he may verbalize as "I worked for what I have. Why don't they?"

Further illustrations could be offered here, but the important point to be made is that consideration or acceptance of even limited aspects of any of these approaches to the underlying factors has a profound effect upon the way human behavior is judged and the manner of the reactions to it.

Social Development of the Economy

Ancient peoples may have prospered through the wise use of resources or the restless development of trade, but attitudes toward work and industry were usually such that they relegated commerce to a low place in the hierarchy of social values. Not averse to enjoying the fruits of economic activity, aristocrats left labor to slaves or the less fortunate; there was no prestige in doing a day's work. When Aristotle spoke for the Greeks of his age in praise of *oikonomia,* the word from which "economy" derives, he meant the careful husbanding of realty and its resources rather than commerce or industry.

The medieval era featured a stable society in which order and regularity generally prevailed. The rules and guidelines set down by temporal and spiritual lords were clearly recognized and people knew their place in the system and what was required of them. As McGuire (1963, pp. 14–18) described them, these were days characterized by stability, security, universalism, and religion. Social values with respect to commerce mirrored many of the earlier views of both the ancient Greeks and Romans. Trade and industry were not discouraged but neither were the attitudes toward them very positive. The Scholastic Fathers of the Church placed commerce last among the professions and their attitudes toward commercial transactions were not such as would encourage economic expansion.

The tremendous outpouring of energies during the Renaissance and Reformation found expansion in commercial channels as they did in scientific and literary endeavors. This period of unrest offered unique opportunities that helped to forge a spirit of individuality and an ethic of achievement. Discoveries and subsequent movements of people loosened the feudal ties, opened avenues of advancement for increasing trade throughout the expanding world, and provided freedom of commerce and merchants within the developing cities. Tillers of the soil who flocked to the city found opportunities to exercise new skills along lines that encouraged self-mastery.

A concomitant development of this time was the growing

emphasis on national identity. Petty lords, previously organized under the feudal system, gradually came to acknowledge a more stable nation-state. This development of European states encouraged activities by navigators and merchants that in turn enhanced the financial well-being and power of the nation. This broad philosophy in which economic activity is considered a tool for national development is known as *mercantilism*. The concepts inherent in mercantilism fitted in nicely with the discovery of new markets, increasing trade, growth of individual freedom, and the development of large cities.

The relationship between religion and economic development also may have been a significant factor in this period. At the risk of oversimplifying, one may say that the Medieval Church, which saw the purpose of activity in this world as the winning of salvation in the next, probably did not encourage commerce. To be sure, capitalism certainly began during the era of the universal Church, the Middle Ages, with the development of trade routes and manufacturing, but historians have placed more emphasis upon the positive relationship between capitalism and Protestantism. Two writers, Weber (1904) and Tawney (1922), are mainly responsible for identifying the close kinship of the values supporting economic development and those espoused in the Protestant Reformation. The emphasis upon individual effort with direct responsibility for outcomes favored the expansion of economic activity. The theology of John Calvin supported capitalism even more in its emphasis upon thrift, hard work, sobriety, and the accumulation of wordly goods that marked one as being predestined for salvation in the world to come. This set of values has become well known as the "Protestant Ethic" and may even be regarded as the essence of the capitalist spirit and the prime moving force for industrial development. In England, Puritanism picked up the values of Calvinism and contributed to "the impatient rejection of all traditional restrictions in economic enterprise which was the temper of the English business world after the Civil War" (Tawney, 1952, p. 226). With the tremendous spurt of technological invention — and perhaps contributing to it — the spirt of independence and accumulation gave the impetus needed for an unparalleled economic growth in the Western world.

This rapid spurt in science and technology had a social impact far beyond the direct economic results. The industrial revolution represents one of the greatest molders of behavior in history as it unfolded in one area of the world after another. The onset of the

17

industrial revolution is difficult to date, as any complex phenomenon inevitably is, although placing the beginnings in the middle of the eighteenth century is as good a choice as any. It was then that the steam engine became available to power a large number of looms, spinning jennies, and other machinery that had been invented within a short period. The need to assemble workers under one roof to tend the expensive equipment surely marked the emergence of the factory, the industrial city, the capitalist system, and the modern corporation. It is true, although perhaps not widely recognized today, that enterprises on a fairly large scale were known as far back as late medieval times — four hundred years before. Brown (1954) describes a cloth factory in France in 1371 employing 120 workers while an English mill not much later had 200 looms and 600 workers. Still, the full bursting of the age of technology did not occur until the period during which the American and French revolutions took place; it continues, with its social concomitants, to this day. The migration from farms to urban areas, the changes in the physical environment, and the socioeconomic tensions are still with us.

Historians consistently have inextricably tied up the industrial revolution with other, more political, revolutions. The social unrest generated by living conditions dictated by primitive responses to the demands of technology has been accompanied by the deprivation felt when political states could not meet certain basic needs of their constituencies. Karl Marx and others responded to the situation in a way that encouraged total and violent reactions, but other contemporaries have exerted their influence upon events through less traumatic means. John Stuart Mill, in an unobtrusive manner, focused attention upon the requirements of human welfare in England through his intellectual furthering of the philosophical positions (the "greatest good of the greatest number") of Jeremy Bentham and the Social Utilitarians. Even Charles Dickens, through his novels, apparently played a role in influencing legislation to ameliorate the civil and economic plight of the nineteenth-century English working classes. Such literary influence was not a new thing for England. Three hundred years before, Thomas More had written in concerned and incisive terms about the social disruption occasioned in that country when small farmers were displaced from the land by the increasing trend away from growing crops and toward the grazing of cattle and sheep on agricultural land. Basic social factors such as these have often been obscured by a concentration upon the influence of personalities, in this case Henry VIII.

In the United States the first real impact of the industrial revolution came in the years immediately following the Civil War. With the rapid expansion of manufacturing facilities, the need for large numbers of workers was met more by immigration than by movement from farms. Later, when restrictive immigration legislation was introduced after World War I, the industrial work force was augmented by farm workers who themselves were being displaced by the impact of science and technology upon agricultural productivity. Fertilizer and farm equipment rapidly cut down the number of people required to raise food for the rest of the population.

In the latter part of the last century the rise in industrial might was furthered not only by the extensive natural wealth of the United States but also by a set of values that fit in neatly with expectations of the developing entrepreneurs. The pattern of beliefs that Max Weber labeled the "Protestant Ethic" encouraged sobriety, hard work, thrift, and individual responsibility. Though originating in the theology of an earlier century, it had dovetailed with the strong thrusts for individual effort and responsibility called for in meeting the challenges of the frontier, and thus flourished on American soil. As a result, this ethic was available as a tradition which not only stimulated the entrepreneurs of the late nineteenth century but also encouraged others to work steadily under the controlled conditions necessary for more efficient output.

If the entrepreneurs, or outright "robber barons," ever had any qualms about their activities they could find some comfort by extending the findings of Charles Darwin to the broader social area. The belief that there is a definite natural law that accounts for the "survival of the fittest" can be adapted to the social scene from the original biological results, much as the English philosopher Herbert Spencer did in Victorian times. The results of industrial development, no matter how ruthlessly attained, could be justified as being in line with one of nature's immutable laws. This basic value orientation is still present to this day, though not always as obviously as in its earlier, cruder forms.

Widespread disregard of the consequences of such orientations upon the quality of personal life and working conditions generated counter reactions tending toward control of economic activity and personnel policies. In much the same way that Dickens pointed out serious deficiencies in the England of his day, many American writers proceeded to shock the conscience of the nation to the point where more positive steps were taken to regulate American industry. Even then, however, there was little concern for the broader effects of industrial activity upon the physical environment. Pollution and population density have only recently become strong areas of concern for a majority of citizens. Up to now, people have proceeded on the simple assumption that air, water, and power were unlimited in quality and quantity.

The Corporation at Present

It is clear that the industrial revolution would never have helped to shape a society in its present comprehensive form without the accompanying emergence of capitalism and the corporation. While it has been suggested that capitalism itself was the force that triggered the industrial revolution, it would not be advantageous to argue the point too far. Suffice it to say that these elements are all part of the same wide structure of events and each has supported the other. Capitalism, which has been described as a system of conflict and competition (McGuire, 1963, p. 26), emphasizes a basic set of values supporting economic activity; additionally, the concept includes the willingness of a number of individuals to contribute their funds (capital) to the launching of an enterprise calculated to provide a financial return on their investment. The sometimes overwhelming preoccupation with a high rate of return and the competitive thrust to attain it has given an unfavorable image to capitalism in the past. Productive business enterprise today expends a great deal of effort to demonstrate concern for a society much wider than the small group of direct investors in the enterprise. Cheit (1964, pp. 152-92), in explaining "why managers cultivate social responsibility," cites numerous instances of the concern of managers for events beyond the confines of the corporation. Despite countless indications in the past of a lack of social service emanating from industrialists, and despite some criticisms of the same sort in present-day life, it is certain that capitalism has made a contribution to contemporary society that few other ideologies can match.

In much the same way the corporation has provided a support for industrial life. The corporate form of activity began because it represented a viable method of organizing the efforts of individuals for more effective action. It remains the most likely medium for achieving individual and group goals despite the real concerns that can be voiced about the power and influence that may be wielded by the corporation in American life. The large corporation is feared not only for the control that it may exercise over economic events, but also for its purported tendency to depersonalize the interrelationships that must take place. Despite these valid questions, however, there seems to be a realization and an acceptance of the inevitability of the corporate form of activity. It exists because it has worked. The corporation has at the very least accompanied the rise of industry and capitalism, if it has not been responsible for its growth. No substitute has functioned quite so well; the question is not whether we should have corporations, but how they shall be administered and how they can relate to the rest of society.

SUMMARY

The lessons of history may lead to a better understanding of present events if they do not lull us into a belief that old responses can always be successful in new situations.

Fundamental views of behavior have conditioned past and present responses to social events. The most basic of these has been the contest between individualism and collectivism. Motivation has been explained in terms of power or pleasure and pain, while determination of the relative effects of heredity and environment has occupied the center of many controversies; looking at individuals according to their status or on the basis of what they have accomplished usually provides differing results. The effect of ideology upon life style has also been postulated.

Ancient peoples generally had a low opinion of commerce and medieval attitudes toward it were scarcely better. Later changes occasioned by travel, discovery, and a breaking of feudal ties provided the energetic base for the Renaissance and more openness to economic achievement. The Reformation and capitalism expanded together with scientific discovery, providing the final boost for the industrial revolution. Entrepreneurs, stimulated by initially favorable attitudes, sometimes exceeded the limits thought socially desirable and eventually came under regulation. Corporate concepts of social responsibility may have emerged from these circumstances but, since the corporate form is here to stay, it is to be hoped that its social consciousness arises from an attitude of concern, rather than merely from compulsion.

BIBLIOGRAPHY

Brown, J. (1954) *The Social Psychology of Industry.* Baltimore: Penguin Books.

Cheit, E. (1964) The New Place of Business: Why Managers Cultivate Social Responsibility. In E. Cheit, ed, *The Business Establishment*. New York: John Wiley & Sons.

McGuire, J. (1963) *Business and Society*. New York: McGraw-Hill.

Tawney, R. H. (1922) *Religion and the Rise of Capitalism*. New York: Mentor, 1952 is the edition used here.

Weber, M. (1904) *The Protestant Ethic and the Spirit of Capitalism*, (trans. T. Parsons, New York: Scribners, 1948).

3

THE "NOW" ISSUES

Inevitably, most contemporary phrases include the word *now*. The Now Generation, Freedom Now, or just an uppercase NOW all point to the power of orientations to the present. But is this characteristic of just the present generation? It may be that each generation has a preoccupation with its own time, and under the pressure of current events easily forgets the past and is not ready to consider the future. To argue the point in order to decide whether our society has more problems or whether we are just more sophisticated in identifying and publicizing them is not a very useful way to face the situations. What is clearly needed is a direct problem-solving response to the issues.

Trying to choose the single most critical problem at this time is also an approach with limited utility. While global questions of how the environment affects the quality of life are important, so are the more immediate and personal ones about the way in which individuals are allowed to develop. Both environmental pollution and a lack of privacy affect the physical as well as the psychological life space of individuals or groups.

Current campus tensions may be one of the better reflectors of present questions about the basic values in our society. If we also ask, as we should, why these tensions are coming to focus at this time, our answers should provide some indication of the source of the greater concern and involvement we see around us.

Keniston (1970) identifies two highly explosive social revolutions. The first of these is the thrust toward equality of opportunity and functioning, the demand for "inclusion" in the industrial society being made by those who have previously been excluded from full participation in the mainstream of society. This group includes not only Blacks but also other ethnic groups, the young, working-class individuals, women, and everyone else who is not a male, white, Anglo-Saxon Protestant.

The second of the two revolutions involves the descendants, primarily the young, of those who have already "made it in the system" and have been reaping the benefits of membership in a favored socioeconomic group. There is in all of this affluence, however, a gnawing feeling of unease about the price apparently paid for its attainment. Even among those who can assume their inclusion in the system there are concerns about the quality of life resulting from it. These feelings have given rise to efforts, some militant and others signifying withdrawal, to achieve more closeness, sensivity to others, and awareness of the challenges to be faced in transforming an impersonal organization or an unhealthy environment into the new forms required.

Individual Rights

There will be little argument that the most fundamental aspect of human functioning is the continuing right to existence. The maintenance of individual freedom and the right to privacy of one's person or thoughts are so basic that even a simulated violation of them, as in George Orwell's novel *1984,* causes apprehension. Concepts such as equality under a legal system or due process of law are supports for this most fundamental and crucial need to exist.

24

The question of freedom is an old one that has often been posed in terms of the antinomy of the individual versus the aggregate as focuses of social orientation, past and present; the person and the collective mark the polar positions. The prevailing values in American history have been, at least professedly, strongly for the individual, although tendencies to curtail individualism in favor of the "the team" or the larger group can be seen in statements advocating more stringent controls, as in many current "law and order" campaigns. In the economic area Skolnick (1965) notes further discrepancies between professed ideals and reality in the fact that Americans consider themselves a nation of individual capitalists, whereas in actuality power is held by large corporations in which only a few people make the decisions. Even philanthropy involves the value judgments of a few who are doing good for others, but on the donor's own terms or in the "society's best interests."

The importance we place on the right to privacy further exemplifies our high valuation of the thrust for individuality. Immediate concerns may be felt in specific situations where employees are subjected to invasion of their privacy through mechanical or psychological means. Surveillance cameras in dressing rooms or psychological tests and polygraph ("lie detector") examinations are techniques that have aroused serious questions or even general resentment in the victims.

The invasion of this fundamental right goes further, however, into broader and more subtle areas. Strong suggestions by administrators to company members with respect to the conduct required off the job, the appropriate place of residence, or even the type of car one ought to drive are not unknown in this day and age. In the not too distant past, some employers were even blatantly paternalistic in personally enforcing codes of conduct for their employees with respect to matters like church attendance or even smoking.

What is and what is not the company's business may be a difficult question to answer, however. One approach suggested (Garrett, 1966) uses a model derived from labor relations, which employs a process of collective bargaining in which both sides agree voluntarily upon the conditions rather than chance the results of unilateral action.

On the broader scene, individual privacy is viewed as one of the foundations of a democratic society (Westin, 1967, pp. 24–26). Where a totalitarian system needs surveillance and disclosure, an open society provides opportunity for expression of ideas, criticism, and consensus on public policy. Individual privacy further provides for the necessary and basic psychological functions of protected communications, self-evaluation, emotional release, and, most of all, the development of personal autonomy. Privacy is an important factor for organizational functioning as well. Quite apart from the collective privacy rights of individuals, organizations must have some freedom from excessive scrutiny if they are to perform as effective units in society. Lack of privacy can hamper organizational autonomy in much the same way as individuals could be restricted by the same lack.

The current demand for equal participation in the political process, the economy, or in education is a further extension of the fundamental right to existence. Identification of the issue with the labels of poverty, welfare, civil rights, and Black studies programs somewhat obscures the basic nature of these as thrusts for existence and the development of personal autonomy. If the posture of businessmen is to consider these problems as updated versions of the older community charity problems and to approach them in the same manner, the efforts at solution are likely to be frustrated. There is no reason why the same amount of effort cannot be expended as before, but the nature of the behavior relevant to dealing with today's problems ought to be well understood.

The claims for representation in the work force are being most strongly pressed by members of minority groups that have been ignored in years gone by. To the ranks of those who have been left out on a racial basis must now be added those who feel discriminated against on the basis of sex. The women's liberation movement contains individuals displaying varying degrees of militancy, just as other minority movements have demonstrated variations in ideology and tactics. All show the same fundamental need for continuing autonomy.

That these events have occasioned surprise in some quarters is in itself surprising. When Gunnar Myrdal (1944) pointed out how the treatment of the Negro was one of the most conspicuous scandals in American society he was only one of many. The pattern of attitudes and beliefs in America on racial matters has been solidly fixed. It may be difficult to comprehend how in 1896 (*Plessy v. Ferguson*) some of this nation's outstanding legal minds could decide that separate facilities for the races would represent equality; it is even more surprising that it was not until 1954 that the death blow for discrimination sounded in the courts. This and subsequent decisions have not solved all the problems, of course, but social progress often comes slowly.

The cataloging of all the outcomes of discrimination would take volumes. The economic losses in untapped human resources are sufficient in themselves to make any society stop to consider whether it was on the right track. When unemployment is twice as high among Blacks as among whites and the buying power of the dollar is smaller (Batchelder, 1965) there is cause for concern for the economy as well as for concern about equality.

Calls for a more active role in the solution of social problems by corporations are being made with increasing frequency. One of the more recent (Fielden, 1970) emphasizes that corporations, if they are to survive, will have to be responsive to the needs of society; they have a tremendous stake in solving problems of employment as well as in community development and have had the potential for accomplishing the task. It is Fielden's contention, however, that this job cannot be accomplished without the help of a new breed of questioning, creative, and innovative members of the organization. Indeed, Fielden believes the very existence of a corporation depends upon its ability to incorporate the dynamic qualities possessed by those who probe the system in an attempt to carry through improvements.

Due process is a legal, conceptual support for the maintenance of individual integrity. The founding fathers of the American republic recognized the importance of the construct and made provision for its incorporation in the Bill of Rights. Later reinforcement of it came with the Fourteenth Amendment which extended the requirements of due process to the states.

More recently, with the growing awareness of the power of "private governments," the concept of due process is being applied to organizations beyond the formal, legal entities to which it is attached on constitutional grounds. It is clear that the functioning of corporations, religious groups, and educational institutions often affects the lives of their constituents more than do the instruments or agents of formal government. If this is the case, it would be of vital concern to society at large to ensure to the members of those private institutions rights similar to those enjoyed by them under formal legal structures.

Potential restrictions on due process in the corporation may arise from the ideology of the "organization man" (Evan, 1961), although countervailing forces may speed the incorporation of procedures preventing arbitrary and unfair actions. Evan sees the development of professionalism and the need for conflict resolution as internal forces which combine with the external pressures from the legal area to extend constitutional safeguards to private organizations.

Further suggestions have been made to aid in the dispensing of justice in the corporation. Some of the most frequent of these call for the inclusion of an *ombudsman* in the company to maintain equitable relationships (Silver, 1967). The possibility of having a highly visible and noteworthy individual to hear aggrieved parties and review administrative actions can stimulate more thoughtful decision-making beforehand and healthier attitudes toward administrative decisions when made. The experience in Sweden from 1906 to date (and in other countries as well) has encouraged the use of an ombudsman system in the "private governments" of this country for "political society has found him to be truly indispensable. In all enterprise, justice *felt* is often justice *achieved*. The corporation, in our time, is a 'dispenser of justice' — both actual and perceived" (Silver, 1967, p. 87).

Economic Power

Business entities, and above all large corporations, are social entities; indeed, by stretching terms a bit, they are even miniature societies. In order to function efficiently the firm must organize the activities of the individuals within it. The social impact of this highly organized activity is very great. A corporation influences not only its members but also many individuals or groups who may not even be in direct contact with it. Unless care is taken, the positive provision of satisfactions for many may be matched by such possible negative factors as disruption of ecological balances in the general environment.

The economic power of the corporation has been analyzed many times over. Berle (1964, p. 102), in one of his last writings on the subject, points out that two-thirds of the productive assets of the United States (which in turn is almost half of the world's manufacturing potential) is in the control of five hundred corporations. This "represents a concentration of power over economics which makes the medieval feudal system look like a Sunday school party." The cause for concern in this area is increased when it is also recognized that decision-making in these organizations is concentrated in the hands of a very few individuals.

The sheer power of economic organizations has given rise to the practice of labeling them "private government." There is no doubt that increasingly the influence of an industrial organization upon the future of one of its members is greater than that of most governmental organizations. When a worker is terminated from company service, the result is often so grave as to be called "industrial capital punishment." Moreover, private governments other than industrial ones may be as important as their industrial counterparts to the future of an individual. The increasingly important role of education makes the college or university a prime source of dissatisfaction or the major contributor to the future development of the entire individual.

The greatest response in a democracy to the fears expressed about "bigness" — in corporations, unions, or even government — has come in the form of support for pluralism. In its emphasis upon the active participation of varied groups in the political process, pluralism reduces the power of any single entity through the competition of many groups for the positions and resources available. This balance of power was the goal envisioned by the framers of the American Constitution as they formed a new government based upon the concept of separation of powers.

The process may be carried further by imposing more controls upon activity rather than simply looking for competing groups to prevent concentration of power. While there may be some latent resentment of control in our society, the anxieties that arise with the possibility of economic control exercised by business or industry have sometimes reached the point where increased governmental power is tolerated to bring the scale of events back into balance.

Anti-trust legislation, regulation of working conditions, or the control of labor-management relations are among the results of this concern for balancing interests on the industrial scene. Still, the approaches have been restrained and agents have refrained from the crude or naked exercise of power to control power. Gossett (1968, pp. 27-28) describes the resulting balances and controls as being "relevant to the democratic unrest. They serve not as rigid braking mechanisms but, so to speak, as cam wheels — permitting complicated and sensitively adjusted movement in a complex social machine where the application of direct power could cause (and has caused in the past) fearful havoc." The fundamental need may be for a stability, rather than a perfect state of equilibrium, in a system that demands effective responses to changing conditions.

There are, of course, other possible means of checking economic power. Among them Friedmann (1957) lists, in addition to anti-trust laws, regulatory agencies, cooperatives, mixed companies, partnerships of capital and labor, or simply social conscience. The more extreme remedies for abuse — involving either mixed public and private enterprise or total socialization of the economy — are quite removed from the mainstreams of thought in our society at present.

Despite the sometimes negative results of its activities, the business firm continues to exist because it provides for the satisfaction of diverse group and individual needs. It is organized to distribute goods and services in an expeditious and efficient manner to persons outside the organization. In the performance of this major function it also serves to satisfy not only the basic physical and security needs of its members but the even more important affiliative, egoistic, and self-fulfillment needs that are often met best in one's occupational life space.

Corporations often list the constituencies for whose benefit they function. There is little argument, at least on the surface, that stockholders, employees, consumers, creditors, or even society at large are included among these constituencies and therefore are to be considered in the decision-making process of the firm. The discussion becomes more serious when some order or priorities among the competing interests is attempted. The necessity of showing a profit is often raised to emphasize the fundamental need for remaining as a functioning entity. The apparent logic of this position is difficult to ignore or refute; a company must be able to stay in business to continue to provide goods and services or income for its members. It may well be, however, that a concentration upon a narrow view of profit obscures the importance to the firm of efficiency in its operations over a longer period of time. The concept of profits, too, should include the non-monetary aspects manifested in the good will or prestigeful position of the company that may accrue through social activity that does not provide an immediate monetary return to the firm. Setting monetary profits of the firm as a goal may be counterproductive in the longer tenure we expect of the corporate form of activity.

Concern for Consumers

When the President of the United States establishes a department to advise him on consumer affairs (killing two birds with one stone by selecting a women to head it) this should be some evidence of the social importance of the area. Additional moves by governors of virtually every state to duplicate this office at the state level confirms the initial impression. Actually, the thrust toward "consumerism" is another of the *now* and *real* issues that are apparent without any close scrutiny of administrative actions. The popular press and the publishing world in general provide much in the way of emphasizing the interest of society in the conditions under which buyers and sellers operate in our present economy.

Concern for the consumer is not an entirely new phenomenon, although the pace of activity certainly has quickened in the last few years of the sixties. In medieval times many sovereign lords, concerned over the price their subjects would have to pay in times of grain shortages, determined maximum market figures. St. Thomas Aquinas, too, discoursed extensively on the notion of "just price." Early modern legislation such as the Food and Drug Act of 1906 represented the beginning of a series of statutes enacted to protect consumer interests. Many of these, however, were drafted quickly in order to provide protection in certain limited spheres of economic activity, so that serious gaps have always remained. The increased concern in recent years has produced some results; in 1962 President Kennedy's special message on protecting the consumer's interests was the first such specific statement ever delivered by a President of the United States on this topic. The succeeding years were increasingly taken up with consumer statutes; an unusual amount of legislation emerged from the 90th Congress in 1967; and even that record year may be surpassed in the near future.

Various rights and duties belong to all parties in the relationship between consumer and producer or between buyer and seller. Even in areas where laws have been enacted to provide for effective social functioning, the statutes sometimes fail to encompass all the ramifications in real situations.

The most fundamental right of individuals in these relationships is, as stated before, the right to existence. Concern for the health, welfare, and safety of consumers should be at the forefront of all activities on the social scene. Drugs, food, automobiles, or almost every other product in use must be manufactured or processed with these considerations uppermost. While little argument takes place on theoretical grounds, problems arise when these concepts are translated into action. How much research and testing must take place before a product is placed in the market? What warnings, if any, are to be included? And when are products to be removed from the market? These are only a few of the questions to be asked. The balancing of risks, costs, efficiency, and social policy is not an easy task.

The right to existence and to autonomy goes beyond the purely physical realm into the broader social area. An individual's economic existence may be hampered by fraud and deception in the product itself or in the terms of the sales agreement. The lack of opportunity or ability on one side to appreciate fully the provisions of a contract may give the other party to it an unconscionable leverage in the relationships. Advertising and promotion, packaging and labeling, and tactics in personal selling all have elements which can cause concern for the rights of consumers.

The impact upon society of these diverse concomitants of consumer activity has been great enough to develop strong thrusts for *consumerism* as the "social force within the environment designed to aid and protect the consumer by exerting legal, moral, and economic pressure on business" (Cravens and Hills, 1970, p. 24). This statement emphasizes again that consumerism is an action along a broad front that includes much more than the formal legal channels. While the new legislation and the attempts of government agencies to implement it cannot be slighted, the more important phenomenon emerging is the activity of private individuals and groups, which is increasing to the point where informal social pressures are overshadowing the slower and more formal legal actions of government bureaus and the courts. At times consumer coalitions or even single individuals manage to put pressure on both government and business to eliminate unethical practices; a Ralph Nader can, virtually single-handed, conduct a crusade for auto safety or proper meat packing procedures. Consumers of the seventies are more educated and affluent, and an additional impetus for action may come from the anxiety stimulated by inflation, from the growing belief that government bureaucrats are unable to effectuate the public interest, or from a general questioning of the "system" or the "establishment."

The above factors and others are usually obvious to even the casual visitor to the market place. Even more subtle and perhaps more influential forces exist, however, in other aspects of consumer activity. The impact of consumer credit, for instance, upon the values and life styles of millions may not be immediately preceived, yet the emergent behavior patterns of a society based upon credit cannot be ignored. A vast change has occurred in the attitudes of Americans, says Caplovitz (1968, p. 641); where "not too long ago, debt was viewed as the mark of the imprudent or poverty-stricken man, today it is part of the American way of life." The results may be viewed as mixed blessings. The status strivings of the middle class now can be met without deferring gratifications, and independence for young families is possible earlier than in the past. At the same time there may be a concurrent upsurge of impulse buying, although some argue that installment credit actually introduces users to proper budgeting principles.

Still further dysfunctional consequences for society lie in the propensity for crimes resulting from the stress to sell or to keep up with the preceived requirements of social status. Caplovitz (1968) has noted a sharp rise in white-collar crime as well as in the numerically greater offenses by and to those in lower socioeconomic levels. That there has been an increase in fraudulent selling practices may be subject to question, but there is no doubt that stronger pressures to own luxury goods and credit cards are a significant part of the social scene. The age-old notions of firm contractual responsibility are giving way to closer scrutiny of activations where unconscionable contracts were entered into as the result of in-equality in bargaining power or the inability of one part to comprehend the conditions. So, too, are we becoming concerned about the plight of those who have become enmeshed in the upward spiral of debt. Garnishment is being looked upon as a less and less necessary way of forcing the payment of a workingman's debts. An all-too-large proportion of the ranks of the unemployed consists of persons who have been discharged by fiscal officers of a company who became impatient with the extra work involved in the garnishment of the work's wages.

In all of consumer conduct, however, there still remain strong feelings of ambivalence. A residue of the Protestant ethic still persists in the concerns about debt, although it is outweighed for the most part by strivings for a status evidenced by the trappings of prestige. Lessons on patience and hard work are countered by the possibility for instant gratification. Being hard-headed and practical in one's affairs often gives way to the more subtle determinants of consumer decision-making that lie in the emotional or affective area. Much of the experience gleaned from marketing suggests, as Levitt (1970, p. 92) points out, that "the customer suffers from an old dilemma. He wants a 'truth' but he also wants and needs the alleviating imagery and tantalizing promises of the advertiser and designer." Perhaps the truth is that those products that are unadorned with seductive blandishments and communicate only sober facts don't sell in the marketplace.

The Environment

Air and water pollution, modification of the climate, solid wastes, noise, radiation and thermal pollution, pesticides, population, land use, diminishing minerals and energy – all are in the forefront of today's discussions. Probably no other domestic issue in the past few years has attracted the attention of the American public or generated as much emotion as has the concern about the quality of life in a rapidly changing environment. Few citizens, if any, oppose the marshaling of energies and resources to improve the conditions of existence; the big rub comes when decisions must be made.

The "Great Environment Crusade," as White (1970) calls it, is stymied by the complexities and the "players in the Environment Game." What exists is a tangle of pressure groups and government bureaus, varying philosophies of government, personal feuds and bureaucratic ambitions, and human failings ranging from apathy to wonderment as to which steps to take to be effective in the political area. At least eighty-four bureaus at the Federal level alone have been playing a role in the mastery of the environment. Overlapping activities and rivalries can be matched by instances where no agency has believed that its charter covered the activity that called for monitoring. This confusing allocation of responsibilities has not made, in the past, for efficient operations. The Water Quality Administration, for instance, is located in the Department of the Interior, while the Air Pollution Control Administration has been placed in the Department of Health, Education, and Welfare. In any case, much positive government action is further frustrated by the continuing shortage of qualified personnel to administer or monitor programs.

But governmental agencies are not alone in the battle. As in the area of consumer protection, private individuals and groups are playing an increasingly active role, even to the extent of including government agents as the targets of their drives to clean up the environment. There is a growing feeling that "agencies are not to be trusted to effectuate the public interest" (Sax, 1970, p. 73) and that government as well as business must be prodded. Litigation by private citizens in environmental matters is becoming the rule where previously a public agency acted as plaintiff in the courts. There is the feeling that government agencies, even if they were alert and responsive, would move too slowly. Since legislatures also react slowly, private plaintiffs are turning to the courts in order to get action while legislators dawdle or to press the legislature into action.

With general agreement as to allocation of resources and proper methods the task would be difficult enough; it looms as a herculean effort in the present circumstances where differing interests collide. For example, farmers undoubtedly are as concerned as others about pollution, but their self-interest may be tied in with the greater use of fertilizers (encouraged by a friendly U. S. Department of Agriculture) that drain off into and despoil rivers and lakes. Industrial plants undoubtedly alter the ecological status quo, but communities may wish to trade increased pollution for the jobs that the new industry brings. The same basic problem exists at a lower level when consumers prefer goods in non-returnable and indestructable containers that can wind up cluttering the countryside.

The general goals may be clear, but how to get there is not. The task calls for administrative skills, certainly, but resolution of the tradeoffs required to gain the objectives stands as the major obstacle.

Urban Life

The placement and movement of people may be considered part of the environmental picture at the same time as it is categorized among the results of poverty, affluence, or economic power. Because it provides a base for discussion of those other aspects, however, the factor of urbanization is important enough to be considered by itself.

As is evident from Chapter 2, urban concentration is not a new phenomenon. The requirements of an industrial economy and the freedom afforded by the city in medieval times provided a clear impetus for the increasing clustering that is still going on. Indeed, the phenomenon has existed since earliest times, leading observers to believe that the growth of cities is a good reflection of the strong social needs in humans. What is new are the precise patterns most recently visible, including that of exodus from a central city to the surrounding suburbs. This is not necessarily a decline in urbanization as much as an extension of the urban sprawl over a larger geographic area, turning outlying areas into a variation of the congestion previously seen only in the urban nucleus. Moving people to the suburbs does not solve metropolitan problems; it only changes their location.

The greater number of people in a relatively restricted space in itself would be enough to provide the basis for increasing urban discord. If we add to this the greater movement of diverse populations and the fact that the city attracts the more active element from these different populations, we can see all the more reason for the deterioration in social relationships. Whether or not there is a "territorial imperative" which causes individuals to resent an intrusion upon their physical life space matters less than the basic fact of friction among diverse peoples coming close together.

It does little good, also, to decry the other conditions of urban life or proclaim that our cities are abnormal. Urbanism is a way of life that is here to stay. What can be done in the situation is the more positive question to pursue.

Social Supports

Much of the past questioning of the role of business entities in promoting social responsibility has taken place as the result of the support by business groups and individuals of community welfare projects in charitable agencies, education, and the arts.

The funding of various charities is nothing new, of course; churches, orphans' homes, and Christmas baskets have long had the warm support of businessmen. In more recent times eleemosynary efforts have become better organized and bigger. Now the United Fund gets attention for its massive effort to cover most, but not all, of the welfare organizations that once competed for contributions in separate fund drives. Programs designed to provide opportunities for individuals heretofore deprived of them within corporate activities are now being considered as the "new charity" (thus glossing over their real meaning). Jobs are being created by the National Alliance of Businessmen and other similar groups and consulting aid is being extended to the minority businessman starting a small enterprise in his ghetto.

Support by business of various endeavors calculated to lift the artistic and educational level of the community is yet another phase of direct action along socially responsible lines. College graduates have long been asked to support their alma mater (and doubtless will continue to be contacted in the future) as their financial aid becomes more crucial, especially for private colleges and universities faced with rising costs and competition for faculty from public institutions. Symphony orchestras, which are seldom self-sustaining, have looked to businessmen for support. Countless other leisure time or recreational activities may also be furthered by the outright generosity or promotional activity of business executives.

But a specific rationale for such participation by corporations has been demanded by those who question the need for such activities.

The demands upon business to move more into a "war on poverty" (and away from military ones) have increased in recent times. To be sure, these suggestions are not new; years ago, in the early stages of the present efforts to alleviate poverty, Galbraith

(1958, p. 331) urged business and society to "invest" in individuals in order to enable them to reach their personal potential, thereby raising the level of the community in which they live, or at least enabling them to leave their immediate environment. Now the number of exhortations to support social programs in hiring or area development are legion; one needs only to pick up any business magazine to see it. How much is being accomplished? Brower and Little (1970) surveyed 281 of America's largest corporations and found that, while the companies endorsed the concept of supporting black capitalism, their total effort was a mere trickle of activity. Part of the problem may be that concern with the security of one's position exists in the minds of executives despite the underlying guilt caused by their lack of action. Carr (1970) responds with a point made frequently in such discussions to alleviate some of this anxiety: If the executive can demonstrate long-range profitability by including social values, he can make his point and benefit in prestige as a result.

There are still, however, those who voice concern, discussed in an earlier chapter, about whether social activism is a proper role for the corporation. At one annual meeting (Standard Oil Co., 1961, p. 15) a stockholder questioned the officers of the corporation with respect to the large donations to charity. "This seems wrong. Your company is supposed to be run solely for the stockholders benefit. . . . Many stockholders undoubtedly feel that charity begins at home." The president of the company responded directly by stating that good corporate citizens must give support to community service organizations from which they expect no direct monetary benefits. Moreover, as we have seen in Chapter 1, such activities can be legally justified by emphasizing the fact that they have always been within the power of corporate executives whose managerial duties included the need to develop the good will of customers and the community; in a complimentary view, McGuire (1965, p. 27) noted that socially responsible corporations do not have higher unit costs when the concept of cost is taken to mean more than a limited, direct dollars-and-cents calculation. When a company is well known in the community for activities that make the community a better place to live, the transfer of this good will to the products can be beneficial financially; customers are often impressed by the concern of the company for the community. Employees, too, may trade a few dollars more in wages for the opportunity to work in a "good" organization.

That these simple factors may even be fundamental and critical in the continuation of business enterprise has been stressed by a few observers. Four decades ago Mayo (1933) argued that those countries whose businessmen turned away from narrow economic profits to more responsible goals would develop in a stable and secure manner while others would experience social disorganization. This may seem a simplistic observation, although there seems to be some evidence to support it.

Despite the criticism of corporate social action, there appears to be little demand for the corporation's withdrawal from this area; on the contrary, the trend is in the direction of stimulating increased effort. If, up to now, corporations have failed to respond to the challenges of a changing environment, say Votaw and Sethi (1969), it is due to the fact that they have not recognized public values as part of their own because they still see the society as composed of independent subsystems rather than as a larger, unified system.

There is hope that all of us, not just those in industrial organizations, will come to realize the fundamental unity of society and the need to consider all its interacting parts.

SUMMARY

A focus on present problems is evident in the interest in getting things done right *now*. Thus concern is expressed both for man's immediate and for his global environment; this concern underscores either the individual or the group psychological and physical requirements in the fundamental need for continuing existence. Thrusts in this direction come from those who have been excluded as well as from those who are uneasy in the fact that they have "made it" at some cost.

Individual rights are those factors that support or further the fundamental right of existence. Freedom, privacy, and equality are aspects of the basic need, while due process and socially responsible acts are procedures whereby these fundamental needs are met. The alleviation of current distress depends upon the effectiveness of the measures that are used to attain the goals set.

The corporation, because of its organized effort, not only has the capacity to satisfy group and individual needs widely, but also has the potential for extensive control. Concern for the negative impact of "bigness" has given rise to consideration of means of regulation. Checks and balances inherent in public government are being extended to these "private governments."

Concern for consumers is increasing, both in governmental agencies and in various private groups that have sprung up to protect the interests of the weaker parties. Questions of health or safety and economic welfare are considered for the benefit of the consumer who, in the end, may be caught in the ambivalence surrounding gratification and restraint in consumption or its financial basis. The state of the physical environment holds the interest of virtually everyone at present. There is little argument about the necessity for attaining a more beneficial setting for functioning, but the welter of competing interests and the complexity of the tasks have militated against an effective, interrelated approach.

Support of artistic, educational, or welfare activities by business institutions has been challenged by some, but ample bases for such activity exist on economic and other grounds. Business activity is part of the total social system and cannot be considered as an independent subsystem without danger to itself and society.

BIBLIOGRAPHY

Batchelder, A. (1965) Poverty: The Special Case of the Negro. *American Economic Review,* 55, 530–39.

Berle, A. (1964) Economic Power and the Free Society. In A. Hacker, ed., *The Corporation Take-Over.* New York: Harper & Row.

Brower, M., and D. Little. (1970) White Help for Black Business. *Harvard Business Review,* 48(3), 4 *et seq.*

Caplovitz, D. (1968) Consumer Credit in the Affluent Society. *Law and Contemporary Problems,* 33(4), 641–55.

Carr, A. (1970) Can an Executive Afford a Conscience? *Harvard Business Review,* 48(4), 58–64.

Cravens, D., and G. Hills. (1970) Consumerism: A Perspective for Business. *Business Horizons,* 13(4), 21–28.

Evan, W. (1961) Organization Man and Due Process of Law. *American Sociological Review,* 26, 540–47.

Fielden, J. (1970) Today the Campuses, Tomorrow the Corporations. *Business Horizons,* 13(3), 13–20.

Friedmann, W. (1957) Corporate Power, Government by Private Groups, and the Law. *Columbia Law Review,* 57(2), 155–86.

Galbraith, J. (1958) *The Affluent Society.* New York: Houghton Mifflin Company.

Garrett, T. (1966) *Business Ethics.* New York: Appleton-Century-Crofts.

Gossett, W. (1968) Balances and Controls in Private Policy and Decision-Making. In G. Hazard, ed., *Law in a Changing America*. Englewood Cliffs, N. J.: Prentice-Hall, Inc.

Keniston, K. (1970) What's Bugging the Students? *Educational Record*, 51(2), 116–29.

Levitt, T. (1970) The Morality(?) of Advertising. *Harvard Business Review*, 48(4), 84–92.

Mayo, E. (1933) *The Human Problems of an Industrial Civilization*. New York: The Macmillan Company.

McGuire, J. (1965) The Social Responsibilities of the Corporation. In E. Flippo, ed., *Evolving Concepts in Management: Proceedings of the 24th Annual Meeting*. University Park, Pa.: Academy of Management.

Myrdal, G. (1944) *An American Delimma*. New York: Harper and Row.

Sax, J. (1970) Emerging Legal Strategies: Judicial Intervention. *The Annals*, 389, 71–76.

Silver, I. (1967) The Corporate Ombudsman. *Harvard Business Review*, 45(3), 77–87.

Skolnick, J. (1965) The Sociology of Law in America: Overview and Trends. *Law and Society. A Supplement to the Summer Issue of Social Problems*, 13(1), 4–39.

Standard Oil Co. (New Jersey) (1961) *Annual Meeting*, May 24, 1961.

Votaw, D., and P. Sethi. (1969) Do We Need a New Corporate Response to a Changing Social Environment? *California Management Review*, 12(1), 3–16, 17–31.

Westin, A. (1967) *Privacy and Freedom*. New York: Atheneum.

White, T. (1970) How Do We Get There from Here? *Life*, June 26, 1970, 38–39.

PART 2

PROBLEMS:
THE INDIVIDUAL
IN THE ORGANIZATION

4

INDIVIDUAL
DEVELOPMENT

The problems in this chapter relate to matters concerning the responsibilities owed to individuals within the organization and, in turn, to the duties members of organizations may have to one another and to the group as a whole. The greatest opportunities for individual development are often to be found within economic organizations; conversely, while the main function of these units may be financial, their potential for satisfying individual needs of all kinds makes corporations among the most important institutions in our society.

It takes very little hunting through the previous three chapters to find the points that must be considered in handling the problems faced within this unit. What is owed by one person to another can be summed up in a set of fundamental questions that have been asked in human relationships since the dawn of history. "Lord, am I my brother's keeper?" has been repeated generation after generation and undoubtedly will continue to be asked through the foreseeable future.

The basic questions often have been raised in subtle ways. When a legal system is based upon concepts of contract, emphasis falls upon individual responsibility in bargaining for the best deal obtainable. If the focus is upon status, the condition of the individual is what determines the outcome. Thus widows and dependent children receive benefits on the basis of what they are and need rather than on the basis of how well they can bargain with others. Differences in approach in this area illustrate basic attitudes and values that have always been present in various societies.

Though it may seem at first glance to be far removed from these matters, the criminal law has similar philosophical bases. Much of what we do in response to crime seems to be in retribution for damage done rather than in order to develop desirable behavior patterns for the future benefit of the individual and society. We often concern ourselves with determining whether the individual was responsible and should therefore "pay," rather than with discovering what course of action will benefit him and society.

The matter of who makes the decisions and how will always remain a problem. Much of the difficulty in society has arisen from the attempts to impose the specific moral code of middle-class decision-makers upon the public at large. The decision of what is "right" or "wrong" is, as we have seen, highly dependent upon social and theological norms and not solely on the abstract principles of the discipline of ethics. We have a tendency to feel that what we do is the natural — or even the only — way to do things. A good decision-maker must be aware of the bases for his decisions and he must be open to alternatives other than those that come immediately to mind; there can be little justification for doing otherwise.

How far must a concern for a specific individual be taken before it collides with the rights of others? A job provides more than money; it is a source of esteem and professional identification. Discharge is a psychologically traumatic experience even when it is not economically catastrophic. A company provides so much support for an employee that any decision of this nature cannot be made lightly. Yet keeping, and in some cases even promoting, individuals who make no contributions to the corporation undoubtedly affects the well-being of others, so that a decision-maker would be remiss in ignoring these factors. Equity is a noble concept in the abstract, but how is it to be achieved?

Perhaps the lesson to be learned from the previous chapters is that one cannot solve problems without both (1) knowing the fundamental bases of our individual and social thought; and (2) trying to translate these basic concepts into real life. Knowing abstract ideas is not enough, although we cannot ignore them in making decisions. Any other procedure would be a mere "bull" session — "rapping" without real purpose.

In continuing discussions with his professional staff, J. Leo Maize, longtime Director of the Accounting Division of the Expro Corporation, emphasized the criteria he used in recommending promotions.

"It's all on merit. If you're good you can go a long way in this office and in the company. Do a good job."

Ted Craig, a personable and capable newer man in the department, took these speeches seriously and turned in excellent performances. He was consistently praised by Maize to the virtual exclusion of others in the department.

When the position of Assistant Director became vacant, Maize announced that Bill Baxter, an undistinguished thirty-year man in the department would be the replacement. Confronted by Craig, about this, Maize explained: "Well, Ted, the old-timers here are a pretty solid group. They've given their professional life to the company and by now they all work well together. A new man would have a hard time with them." Maize neglected to mention that both he and Baxter belonged to the same church and that they had played bridge in the same club for years.

*　　*　　*

1. What can Craig do?
2. What are possible outcomes of any step Craig takes?
3. What are Maize's responsibilities to the company? Has he met them?
4. What are the company's responsibilities to Craig?
5. What would have been the probable result had Craig been given the promotion?

At the Wanco Corp., a producer of kitchen appliances, the position of Manager of Personnel Systems and Procedures was suddenly vacated by the resignation of the first incumbent of the office since a recent reorganization. This slot has been a critical one in the table of organization inasmuch as the Personnel Systems and Procedures office reviews the staffing of all positions and the development of procedures in each department of the company.

E. R. Bragg, the executive vice president, after a series of interviews with candidates inside and outside the company, approached B. B. Maxwell, the president, with his suggestion for filling the position. "The best of the lot is Jim Topen."

"Well," rejoined B. B., "you make the hiring decision."

Topen was hired and one week later it came to the attention of the president that Topen was the nephew of Bragg, the executive vice president who made the decision.

"Why didn't you tell me before we hired him that Topen was your nephew?" said Maxwell.

"But B. B.," responded Bragg, "he's the best man. It makes no difference that he's a relative of mine."

* * *

1. Should Bragg have done anything differently? If so, what?

2. Did Bragg have a duty to disclose his relationship to Topen?

3. To whom should disclosure have been made? Would it have made a difference?

4. Does the nature of specific position in question make a difference in viewing this problem?

The Fina Furniture Company prided itself on the craftsmanship that had always gone into its products. For a century the label Fina was synonomous with high quality. Most of the work was hand executed, from start to finish.

Beauregard Ravenal, Jr. ("Young Bo"), took over the reins of the company upon the death of his father, affectionately known in the company as "Old Bo." Fresh from a graduate program in business administration, Young Bo recognized that the company was in a poor financial situation and that immediate positive steps had to be taken. He decided to automate the major operations and to develop deisgns calling for greater use of veneer and urethane figuring.

"But Mr. Ravenal," protested the plant superintendant, "many of our craftsmen will lose their jobs and they're at an age where it will be difficult for them to find work. And what will happen to the company image we've been careful to build?"

There was a general feeling in the company and community that Old Bo would never have considered such courses of action.

*   *   *

1. Could Young Bo justify his decision? How?

2. What responsibilities, and to whom, did Fina have in these circumstances?

3. What is the likely result of Young Bo's decision for the craftsmen?

4. What will be the impact of his decision upon the community?

Dr. Carl M. von Weber has been widely regarded as one of the leading solid state physicists in the country. In his twenty years with the SPD Electronics Corp. he has been primarily responsible for the success of the commercial applications projects undertaken by the corporation. These projects have accounted for 10 percent of the activity of the company, while the remaining 90 percent of the effort has been expended on government contracts. Dr. von Weber's experience had never been needed on the relatively unsophisticated military contracts so far received.

In the fluctuating world of government contracting the company periodically faced liquidation. Now, after great effort and anxiety, company officials learned that their proposed bid on the "Neutra" developmental contract (that would provide economic security for at least five years) was likely to be the winner.

A week later the company's Washington representative called the president on the phone: "We don't get to bid on the Neutra contract with von Weber on it. He can't get security clearance. At age 18 he was a member of the Youth for a Free Westphalia, a Communist-front organization."

On checking with the executive vice president it was learned that the company was relying on von Weber to direct the project. "Can we do it without him," asked the president. "We can try," said the research director, "but it doesn't look good."

"The charge is unfair nonsense," said the company lawyer. "We could fight it and win, but by then we would have lost the contract. It's better for von Weber to accept the finding."

* * *

1. If no contest is made on the charge, how does this affect von Weber?
2. What are von Weber's duties to the company?
3. What does the company owe von Weber in this situation?
4. If the company goes ahead without von Weber, what might be the result?
5. What are the probable outcomes for the country?
6. Are there any other parties not specifically mentioned here who would be affected by the decision?

Stan Strate was one of the younger staff men working in the accounting department of the Wispro Corporation. By virtue of his substantial training and experience in the use of electronic data processing techniques for the corporation's accounting processes, he was one of Wispro's most valuable employees. Strate's immediate superior, Bill Oldham, was particularly concerned about losing Strate because there was no one else in the department, including Oldham, who could cope with the EDP work.

Oldham's anxiety mounted to a high level when he received a call from an accountant friend who worked for a competing company: "Bill, you're a friend of mine so I want to clear it with you first. That young man Strate in your department is interested in joining our company. OK with you? What's your opinion of him."

Restraining himself somewhat, Oldham replied: "Well, we don't want to keep a man here if he thinks he can improve himself. He's good at his work. I can recommend him. Oh, he sometimes rubs people the wrong way — you know how it goes sometimes."

Annie Lee, Oldham's secretary, overheard these statements. "Mr. Oldham," she said, "Stan is one of the nicest people here. I don't know anyone who dislikes him."

*   *   *

1. What was Oldham trying to do?
2. How could Oldham justify his actions?
3. What should Annie Lee do in this situation?
4. Is there any other way Oldham might have proceeded?
5. What duties does Oldham have with respect to Strate?
6. Could the inquiring executive have proceeded in another way? What consequences might have resulted?

Ned Harrigan, a young accountant for the Wenatchee and Memphis Railroad, received high ratings for his work at company headquarters for the year he was with the company.

In this even numbered year, the state and nation were engaged in active political campaigns.

One morning Ned found a pledge card for the Magnolia County Democratic Party in his mailbox. Upon inquiry he ascertained that these cards had been circulated by the administrative assistant to the vice president.

When Ned's card was not returned, the Office Manager came around to collect the pledge.

"But I'm not even a member of that party," complained Ned. "That's okay," said the office manager. "Contribute to that other party, too."

When Ned was still reluctant to contribute, he was called into the vice president's office to explain why he had not made a pledge. On returning to his office without contributing, he was told by the office manager:

"You're making this office look bad, Ned. You should know that the vice president approves all promotions. Make the contribution and submit the sum on a voucher as an expense on a business trip."

* * *

1. When the issue was put to him as it was, should Ned have contributed?

2. What is the effect of submitting the sum as a business trip expense?

3. Would your response to this problem have been different if the manager had not suggested including the contribution as a business expense?

4. If there were no insistence upon contributions to a *specific* political party, how would you react?

5. What is Ned's "duty to the team"?

6. Suppose the recipient in this case were the United Fund? What would your responses to the foregoing questions be? Why?

7. Are there any other situations where similar actions would take place?

Tom Hastie was a bright young student at the Manhattan Institute of Technology who received many fine offers of employment in his senior year. He was particularly attracted to the Intersystems Electronics Corporation (IEC), in part because of their liberal policies on employee education programs. He accepted the job with IEC upon graduation and after six months as a management trainee he found out that the company was even willing to grant him leave at 50 percent of salary so that he could pursue full-time graduate work at a prestigious Eastern school of business administration. In addition, the company paid all tuition and fees each semester as he registered. There was no oral or written agreement entered into at any time as to the continuation of employment with the company after receipt of a graduate degree, but all such student-employees in the past had taken returning to their jobs at IEC as a matter of course.

Tom received his MBA and, after a two-week rest, notified his last immediate superior at IEC of his intention not to return to his original post with the company. He stated that he could not turn down a "challenging" offer (more money) made to him by one of IEC's competitors while he was in the final months of his MBA program.

"Tom" said Paul Jenkins, his immediate supervisor in the company, "we were counting on you to come back and help us in the Ajax project. We need you very badly."

*   *   *

1. What were Tom's legal obligations?

2. Is Tom likely to recognize any duties other than legal ones?

3. If Tom were criticized for his move, what do you think he would say in his defense?

4. Is the fact that in the past all employees in Tom's situation returned after graduate work binding upon anyone?

5. What could company officials do in this situation? Would they do anything?

5

EQUALITY
AND PRIVACY

Strong thrusts for participation in the social, educational, and political processes represent vital forces in our society. Concomitant moves toward the preservation of individual integrity through privacy and freedom present the complementary side of the picture, with their concern for individual autonomy. As with most problems, positions that are clear when stated in the abstract may be much less so when actual concrete situations must be faced. The interplay of various forces in society may alter conclusions arrived at under other conditions.

No one can doubt the widespread agreement in our society on the need for equality of treatment for all persons. The civil rights movement emphasizes what is now considered to be a cornerstone of our democratic society — full participation in the political and social processes of the country. Contemporary notions of morality or ethics support these basic positions, even though it must be remembered that broad acceptance of the concept of real equality is of fairly recent vintage. Each era has had groups that defined the membership, so that all members were equal only in the light of their definitions. Even the egalitarian founding fathers of our Republic restricted the rolls of voters to male holders of real property; it didn't matter how much you had in the bank — if you didn't own land you didn't vote. Women never made it to the polls nationally until the preceding generation.

In practice, there have been other limitations that have been just as significant though more subtle. Blacks sometimes have been subjected to rigorous tests of knowledge of statutes in order to qualify as voters. Attitudes favoring a subordinate role for women have tended to keep all but the most active females away from top decision-making sessions in the political area. Over and above this, the poor and the less well-educated seldom have the time, ability, and inclination to participate as actively as those who have had many opportunities to do so in the past or have been encouraged to play major roles in society. George Orwell's aphorism that "some are more equal than others" really means that some are more *active* than others and, often by virtue of this fact alone, have more influence over the course of community events.

When we leave the public sector and come to other, more private areas, the question of participation may be even more important. Economic participation is a "gut" issue in more ways than one, for the most basic physical factor of survival may be involved, as may the psychological foundation for identity and self-respect. The highly influential role of private enterprise corporations in our society has been emphasized repeatedly. Clearly they are so important in our lives that distinctions between the public and private sectors may be misleading. Indeed, this difference may even disappear as we adapt to environmental changes with new organizational forms of activity. For some to argue, then, that such "private" relationships are not to be considered in reviewing governmental or outside agencies does not seem justified in the light of practical outcomes. The industrial company is apt to have more immediate meaning for, and control over, its members than most agencies of government.

Even with agreement on abstract concepts and how widely they can be applied, the practical applications of decisions raise difficulties. Our system is one great zero-sum game in which giving something to one group means that it is taken away from another set of individuals. When this happens, even in the framework of "causing inequality by making up for previously unequal conditions," the furor among these slighted is undoubtedly great. To believe that these circumstances are based solely on monetary considerations is to relate to surface factors in a misleading way, for economic conditions also involve basic security, identity, and prestige needs of individuals. Thus the reactions to any threat in these areas is apt to be strong.

Education, too, has always been important inasmuch as it has been the base for further significant activity in society. When job requirements call for educational credentials (whether justified or not), the possession of these credentials is a factor in the selection of people for positions which will offer no opportunity for testing performance on the job.

Nor can we, even at this point in history, throw away the social and psychological accretions built up over past centuries. Our feelings about the "proper way" represent myriad basic attitudes and values passed on to us. The various threads of thought in Chapter 2 are recognizable in all our positions taken on topical issues. Do we expect each person to stand on his own abilities and be responsible for his own actions or do we extend aid by virtue of his position in society or his need at a particular time? Are we "our brother's keeper" or does he have to look out for himself? Some people provide their society with more benefits than others, and we have always rewarded and respected those who contributed more to their community. To what extent can we ignore such differentials in the contribution made to society? Finally, in any disparity between group and individual goals or requirements, how much concern for individual rights can be present when a threat to group welfare is said to exist? These and other fundamental questions have been with us for a long time.

Privacy is one of those individual requirements for continuing existence and autonomy. Each of us, even though we are social beings, attempts to reserve some part of his psychological and physical life space to himself, although doing so may be getting more difficult all the time as the expansion in population proceeds apace with increasing sophistication in technological devices that invade privacy without the victim's awareness. In any organization an individual may feel that his need for some autonomy is greater than the demands placed upon his time and effort by the group. The inevitable stresses of the situation provide many of the problems of contemporary society when the two conflicting pulls on the person cannot be resolved effectively. Indeed, in all interpersonal relationships the ambivalence between the desire to exchange confidences or participate in society on the one hand and to keep things secret on the other is a continuing source of difficulty in personal functioning. The holder of confidential information carries a heavy burden for many reasons, including the power it gives him over the individual who has confided the information. A knowledge of secret weak spots enables one to control or manipulate, as many once-intimate interactors have discovered.

In summary, it must be stressed again that the problems dealt with in this chapter may be identified in such familiar terms as *equality, privacy, identity,* or *freedom,* but no real understanding accrues simply for applying these labels. The serious student of social problems must go below the surface to identify what these words really mean.

Jack Demmler, the manager of the Environmental Systems Division of ZUCO was at his desk trying to catch up on his paperwork when one of his foremen, Stan White, burst in. (Demmler prided himself on his "open door policy.")

"What the hell are you people trying to do?" shouted White. "I just read in the morning paper that you're going to hire forty no good bums off the street while my boy who wants to work here with me has been waiting six months for a job without being hired. He's smart — had one year of college — and he served in Vietnam with honor. Why can't he get a job?"

"Stan, these are not bums we're hiring," responded Demmler; "they're hard-core unemployed. We have a social obligation to give them a chance." Demmler might have added, but did not, that he had received orders from ZUCO headquarters to hire these men. ZUCO officials accepted a quota of "hard-core unemployed" to be distributed among their plants as the result of volunteering to do so under HELP (Hard-core Employment Labor Program), an association of businessmen.

"Social obligation be damned!" sputtered Stan as he stormed out of the office.

*   *   *

1. What is the extent of the social obligation of the company?
2. What might be the effects of such policies upon the company, its employees, the community?
3. What is the state of the labor market at this time?
4. What justification does HELP have for its program?

C. Jackson (Jack) Smith served the Expro Corporation in several personnel capacities for over twenty years. His ability was acknowledged widely in the company, so it occasioned little surprise when Smith was named as the replacement for the retiring Manager of Personnel for the Corporation.

When the appointment of Smith was announced, the response from certain segments of the community was unexpectedly negative. Announcing that he was a "representative of the black community" in the city, Floyd Davis confronted the president of Expro: "Jack Smith has a long history of racism. He has been biased in his personnel decisions, and his emphasis on racially biased I.Q. tests for prospective employees has kept Expro from hiring its proper share of black workers. We demand that you reconsider his appointment."

The president solicited the opinions of others in the company. It was their opinion that Smith had been singled out for this attack even though he was only following employment policies that were not out of the ordinary in industry. All company officers contacted felt that Smith was doing a good job and that there was no evidence of racism.

Floyd Davis, as well, was adamant in his stand.

*   *   *

1. Is there any basis for the stand taken by Davis?
2. What is likely to happen if the company reconsiders the appointment?
3. What could happen if the company refused to reconsider?
4. How can the company support its decision to appoint Smith?
5. What are the duties of the company to Smith?
6. What are Smith's responsibilities in this situation?

Ingeborg's Restaurant in Central City was, for many years, an undistinguished eatery which featured a Swedish Smorgasbord. Finally, to try to boost its reputation and sales, the owners hired André Flamboyante, a restaurant manager who had a national reputation for developing and maintaining fine restaurants.

"The important thing," said André to the owners, "is that a central theme must be maintained, both in the food and in the surroundings. Running a restaurant is an artistic endeavor that appeals to all the senses. The restaurant must be true."

The restaurant was redecorated at considerable expense with artifacts from Sweden to make it authentic. Flamboyante chose his waitresses carefully to conform with the basic theme. Some even came from Sweden.

The results were even better than the owners forecast and business reached the point where reservations were necessary in order to dine at Ingeborg's. Success led to expansion until there was a chain of Ingeborg restaurants in many surrounding states.

A year after the reopening Sally Jones, an attractive, young, black college sophomore applied for a position as waitress in order to earn money to continue in school.

"Well, my dear, you're lovely," said André, "but we can't use you."

Three days later Flamboyante received a call from the attorney for Civil Rights Now: "Miss Sally Jones will file a complaint alleging violation of the Civil Rights Act of 1964."

"I'm sorry," said André, "but we are not in violation of the statute. It is important that we remain true to ourselves and to our art."

*   *   *

1. What justification is there for André's saying that there was no violation of the statute?

2. Are there any considerations that take precedence over the artistic?

3. Do you have any positive responses to counter the arguments for authenticity?

4. Did Ingeborg's Restaurant have any responsibility in this matter to Sally Jones, the community, or to anyone else?

Cogit and Co. is a well known management consulting firm operating throughout the Western world. Zapco, Inc., a heavy-duty highway equipment manufacturer, has utilized the services of Cogit and Co. in various personnel and production situations during the past several years.

In each report the consultants emphasized the somewhat tenuous nature of their findings; this was attributed primarily to the fact that the work activity being observed was undoubtedly atypical because of the highly visible presence of the team of consultants with their data-gathering apparatus. Each report suggested that a less obvious set of techniques be used.

When the company experienced some difficulty in the X-50 Earthmover Assembly Department, the president finally agreed that the members of the Cogit team would come in as "participant observers" — that is, they would join the company along with new employees and be put on the job without the other workers knowing the real identity and function of the consultants.

*   *   *

1. What rights are at issue here?
2. What are the responsibilities of Zapco?
3. If you were a foreman and aware of the situation, what would you do?
4. Would your answer be different if the team used surveillance devices rather than just observed work?

Albert Grimes worked for twenty years as an accountant for the Micro Company. His immediate superior, Wm. Budd, annually rated him as above average even though Grimes would occasionally exasperate others by his insistence upon following company accounting procedures to the letter.

One morning Budd found out that Grimes had been picked up by the police the night before in a raid on a disorderly house.

"But I'm innocent," pleaded Grimes. "All I did was go there, next door to my place, to complain about the noise. The police arrived just then."

Budd talked to the president of the company. "This is a small town and whether or not Grimes is guilty it will have a bad effect on our image. I'm going to tell him to forfeit the bond. It won't get any publicity that way."

"I will not," sputtered Grimes. "I'm innocent and I'll prove it in court."

The charge against Grimes was eventually dismissed but not until the local newspaper featured every incident of the case. On page twelve at the end of the news story was the following paragraph: "The charge against one of the defendants, Albert Grimes, an accountant at the local Micro plant, was dismissed for lack of evidence." Budd again went to the president. "We should fire Grimes for not being willing to save himself and the company from embarrassment."

* * *

1. What are the rights of Grimes in this situation?
2. What support has Budd for his position?
3. Would the company be justified in releasing Grimes? If not, what could it do?
4. Suppose Budd were visited by a group of women from Grimes' office who said they were ashamed to work in the same office with Grimes. What should Budd's stand be?
5. If the women said they feared for their safety with a man like Grimes, what would be your counsel to Budd?

Scruffy Products, Inc., is primarily a marketer of products used in the home. Recent rapid growth of the company has been attributed to a great extent to the vigorous efforts of its president, B. J. Smith. B. J. himself has given much of the credit to the program for selecting salesmen in the field. The outstanding success of this approach precipitated the following notice:

> To: All Headquarters' Staff
> From: B. J. Smith
> Subject: Personality Tests
>
> Starting on March 1, all members of the staff and their wives will take the personality tests to be administered by our staff psychologists. Your cooperation will be appreciated.

Response to this memorandum was not slow in coming. In the accounting department Edgar Owlish, an accountant with fifteen years of service, walked right into the office of his superior.

"Mr. Grant, this is the most reprehensible thing I know of. No head shrinker is going to probe into my private life. What I do after hours is my own business — and stay away from my wife, too."

"But Edgar, this is something that has helped to build the company to its present strong financial position. All the salesmen we have now took this test."

*   *   *

1. Is Edgar on solid moral ground in his objection?
2. Does he have any other bases for objecting to the testing?
3. Suppose the company wants to test only Edgar and not his wife? Does this make a difference?
4. What are Edgar's rights and what recourse does he have?
5. What does Edgar owe the company?

Rodney Sikes, Ph.D., was a clinical psychologist engaged in private practice before being hired by the Progressive Engine Co. as the staff psychologist and counselor. The idea of employing a psychologist to counsel employees was generated from a series of courses attended by the president of Progressive at a well known "personal development center" on the West Coast.

Initial suspicion or even hostility was slowly overcome by the patient posture of Dr. Sikes and his often repeated statement concerning the inviolability of the client-counselor relationship. Confidentiality was not to be breached. Gradually employees began to drop by Sikes' office to "talk things out."

A recent visitor, displaying some anxiety symptoms, was Bill Smith, assistant to the chief of the Accounts Payable section. It developed that Smith has known, but has kept silent, about a successful plan of the chief of the section to siphon funds into his bank account under a fictitious name in another city.

"Gee, I feel better already," said Smith, "but don't tell anybody else about this."

*   *   *

1. Would Sikes be justified in violating confidentiality in this situation?

2. What criteria can Sikes use to determine whether disclosure is justified?

3. Does the request by Smith have any validity? Should Sikes respect it?

4. What might some of the results of disclosure be?

5. What could the results be if Sikes keeps quiet?

6. To whom does Sikes owe the highest duty?

7. Are there any other alternatives besides disclosure and keeping silent that might be pursued?

Clem Jones was an Assistant Director of Personnel for the Chimera Corporation. His main task was to develop and execute selection procedures for managerial, clerical, and skilled positions in the company.

Jones' latest effort was a long-overdue revision of the application blank — changes that were called for in the light of empirical and legal information available to the Personnel Department.

When Jones turned his finished product over to M. R. Jenkins, the Director of Personnel, the response was rather strong:

"You'll have to take this question that asks the sex of the applicant out of the form. I have problems enough with the women's liberation groups without getting into a mess on this."

"But M.R.," replied Jones, "this doesn't violate the law. I have a very valid basis for including the question in the form."

*   *   *

1. What might have been the reasons for changing the application blank?

2. What basis might Jones have for including the question?

3. What response might be made to Jones?

4. Are there valid grounds for Jenkins' response?

5. What is more likely than sex to be a problem for the drafter of an application blank?

6. Respond to questions 2, 3, and 4 in terms of your answer to question 5.

6

ROLE REQUIREMENTS

An individual within an organization frequently finds himself in situations where his role is unclear or, even more unsettling, where multiple requirements come into conflict. The unease or anxiety generated by the lack of clear guidelines may lead to ineffective or even counterproductive responses. The stress of competing requirements or loyalties may develop more discord than clean-cut opposition could.

In the problem areas to be considered here, some of the very same questions that have been discussed in the preceding problem chapters arise again, this time with additional facets to keep in mind. When there is competition for the loyalties of the decision-maker, the number of relevant factors at least doubles, with each factor having its conflicting questions of responsibility or morality.

Conflict of interest has been a problem since man emerged from the simplest society, in which each person played only one major role. With the increasing complexity of society, the opportunities for multiple roles and for conflict between them increases as well. Change, too, adds uncertainty; whereas formerly ethical problems would have been handled, for better or worse, in traditional ways, today's new conditions provide new problems with new ethical connotations for which the older guidelines may not be effective.

The broad patterns that develop in a larger society are usually mirrored in the functioning of organizations within it. At times the structure of the industrial firm is such that uncertainty about roles and subsequent procedure is common. A subordinate who reports daily to one supervisor (who may be the decision-maker in promotions) yet has the responsibility of monitoring the supervisor's fiscal activities and reporting to higher headquarters is clearly in a bind. With the further absence of stated policy or specific procedures to be followed, the responses of members of the organization are apt to be variable and often anxiety-producing, primarily because no one can predict what will happen next. There can be no security without the stability that comes with a certain measure of predictability of behavior in a given situation. Not knowing what to do becomes even more upsetting when the behavior is invested with the strong emotional components of activity that a society calls "right" or "wrong," "ethical" or "immoral," etc.

In many contemporary problems there may be little question that decision-makers wish to do the "right" thing. What is missing, however, is a fuller evaluation of the many alternative courses of action or the impact of these on the constituencies involved. Instead of such an evaluation there is often only a simple hierarchy of interests with consideration, in the press of everyday activity, of only the problems and people that are prominent in the executive's thinking. Other aspects often get lost in the shuffle. In this and subsequent chapters, the problem-solver will be required to consider more and more aspects of the problems posed and the possible ramifications of the proposed solutions. Only in this way can the really critical issues be faced.

For many years Bill Bixby has been the advertising manager for the Independent Amalgamated Grocers of Ohio (IAGO), a large network of affiliated grocery stores. At a quarterly meeting of the Board of Directors of IAGO, one of the directors informed the others that many sales managers of soap companies were annoyed by the preferential treatment accorded Fluffo soap in all the advertising put out by the association. The Board asked the chairman to check on the situation.

After some investigation, it was discovered that Bixby had a credit card under which Fluffo was billed directly. When Bixby was confronted with this he replied:

"Sure, but Fluffo does this for others, not just me. Besides that's not the reason I included it in our ads. It's bio-degradable and contains no phosphates to add to the water pollution problem."

The Chairman pointed out that the cost of Fluffo to IAGO members was higher than that of other soaps but that the advertised price in the ads meant a mark-up at retail that was smaller. In this way Fluffo was made competitive in price with other soaps.

* * *

1. What is payola?
2. What duty did Bixby have to IAGO? Did he violate it?
3. What justification could Bixby have for his policies?
4. If Fluffo did not cost IAGO members more, would this make a difference?
5. If Bixby had no credit card from Fluffo, would this have made the situation different?
6. Fluffo treats other ad managers in the same way. Does that make a difference?

The Board of Directors of the Brand X Corporation was meeting in regular session. All members were in attendance because the Board is composed of "inside" directors — that is, all of them are active officers of the corporation.

"I move we grant additional stock options in this fiscal year to those executives of the corporation who qualified under our previous plan to the extent specified by that plan," was the motion by the Financial Vice President.

"Seconded," said the Secretary.

In the limited time available for discussion on the motion, various members spoke to the issue. A few remarks pointed to the financial state of the corporation and the tight money market. Other speakers reflected upon the needs met by the improvement of the stock option program.

*   *   *

1. What are the needs met by the stock option program?
2. What other benefits are there?
3. What might be the effect upon the stockholders of a "yes" vote?
4. Are there any deleterious effects of the move?
5. Suppose the Board voted instead to declare substantial dividends to stockholders. What would be the impact of this move?

Mark Sensor was employed by Tabco, Inc. in the Data Processing Systems Division. He came to the job well recommended and generally performed at an acceptable level. Occasionally, however, a machine routine supervised by Sensor would cause problems and delay the operations of the division. The difficulties encountered seemed to be traceable primarily to simple questions of judgment. Harold West, the Division Manager, decided there might be some lapses of attention to work on the part of Sensor.

When it came to West's attention that Sensor was working six hours daily on a job after his working hours with Tabco, West sent for him.

"Mark, I hear you're working at another job after hours here."

"That's right, sir. I need the money. There's no rule against it, is there? I don't know of any."

* * *

1. Working on a second job after a regular, full-time job is called moonlighting. What are some possible effects of moonlighting?

2. How can Sensor support his actions?

3. What does Sensor owe Tabco?

4. Are there any duties owed by Sensor to the second company?

5. What are the possible effects of this moonlighting activity on Sensor?

6. What should West do?

In a large public accounting firm one of the young accountants recently recruited from college was engaged in supporting his proposal for handling a new account.

"With respect to our fee, we should be flexible in this case. This community service organization is having a hard time getting started and they can't survive without help. In six months they should receive a government grant and we will certainly be in a good position to get their business then."

"Good heavens, no," rejoined the supervisor. "Do you want to get us into trouble with the American Institute of Certified Public Accountants (AICPA)?"

The Code of Professional Ethics of the Institute states in article three:

3.02:   A member or associate shall not endeavor directly or indirectly to obtain clients by solicitation.

3.03:   A member or associate shall not make a competitive bid for a professional engagement. Competitive bidding for public accounting services is not in the public interest, is a form of solicitation, and is unprofessional.

"If one provision doesn't cover this case, the other one does," stated the supervisor.

*   *   *

1. What arguments could be made for providing a free consulting service?

2. What are some of the effects of adhering to the provisions of this code of ethics in this case?

3. Why would a professional organization promulgate these provisions in a code?

4. What is solicitation? Give examples. Could you outline arguments in favor of and against this practice?

5. If a code of this kind is violated, what might be the results?

One of the new salesmen in the company was discussing some of his problems with one of the old-timers on the sales staff.

"That entertainment allowance we get is, believe it or not, pretty hard to spend during the day. I could take a lot of my customers out at night, too, and there would be no trouble getting through it, but I want to spend time at home. My family needs me."

"Let me clue you, kid," replied the old-timer. "That allowance helps to make up for the fact that our base salary is lower than our competitor's. None of us spends much of it on entertainment and you don't have to either. We deserve the extra money. The company gives it to us whether we spend it on customers or not. We all pocket it."

*   *   *

1. What does the company require of its salesmen under these circumstances?

2. What does the company owe the salesmen?

3. Is there any way in which the salesmen, in following the practice described by the old-timer, are derelict in their duty?

4. Are there any other aspects of the situation that should be considered?

5. Is there an ordering of priorities with respect to the parties to be served by the salesman? In other words, who comes first — company, customer, family, etc.?

6. All the salesmen do it. Why should anyone be concerned?

The expenditures of each sales division of Simco, Inc., are monitored by the Central Accounting Office of the corporation. Each sales division has a budget control officer who reports directly to the Central Accounting office even though he is a subordinate of the division manager.

When the report for the first quarter was coming due, the Snowshoe Division budget control officer, Stanley Subb, approached Sam Super, his division manager.

"Mr. Super, the expense accounts of Lola Goetz, your special assistant, have been very extensive in the past few quarters. This quarter it's even higher and I'm afraid that I can't send it in without saying something."

"Listen, Subb, I've told you repeatedly that Miss Goetz is in charge of special promotions. Because of this she has larger expenses than the others do, but she is invaluable to our sales effort. Send the voucher through," emphasized Super.

Subb was placed in a dilemma. On the one hand he was responsible for the evaluation of all expenditures before sending the valid ones to the main office. He was, however, administratively under Super, who participated in personnel decisions affecting Subb and other divisional employees.

*   *   *

1. What is the basic problem in this case?

2. What can one do to avoid difficulties in this connection in the future?

3. What should Subb do at this time?

4. Suppose Subb hears rumors of a close after-hours relationship between Miss Goetz and Super. Does this make a difference in what Subb should do?

Walter Wright, a recent graduate of Overshoe State College, finished the Management Training Program of the Wispro Corportion and was assigned to the Fabricating Division's main plant. There he was named the Production Supervisor of the Relay Assembly line. Wright was thought to be a bright young man and inasmuch as the Relay Assembly had never experienced severe problems or major fluctuations in production levels, it was considered a good spot in which to start a new man.

In his first week at the new job. Wright noticed many discrepancies between actual production situations and the recorded figures. Finished units were sometimes logged under a different work shift, production was credited to later periods in the month, and various workers were allowed to save credits for later slack periods.

Wright called in his chief foreman, Stan Firme, and stated: "I'm going to run this place as it should be run — by the book. I learned in the training program that the company spent many hours developing the right system and they want it followed. Giving them the wrong info is unethical."

$$* \quad * \quad *$$

1. The later posting of earned credits in production is usually referred to as stockpiling. Why does it occur?
2. What are the results of stockpiling?
3. Is this system unethical?
4. What response might company executives make if they became aware of it?
5. What would be the results of a move to stop it or of disclosure by Wright?

Bill Marshall returned home from an out-of-town business meeting in a somewhat agitated state. "Bill, you're jumpy, what's wrong?" his wife asked. In all their twenty years of marriage Bill Marshall had never kept secrets from his wife not even those affecting the company, so after two martinis he proceeded to relate what he discovered on the way home from the meeting.

Bill rode back with a fellow executive, Jim Simpson, who was head of the Transformer Division and thus was neither a superior nor a subordinate of Bill's. During the course of the trip Jim gave Bill the impression (but did not say so directly) that he, Jim, and others in the Transformer Division periodically participated in "conversations" with competitors in the same industry. Bill had heard before that such secret meetings resulted in elaborate formulas to govern the bidding by each company so that contracts would be distributed to each without the companies having to compete strenuously with each other. Bill told him he was "a damn fool" for participating in such obvious violations of the Sherman Anti-Trust Act.

"Mary, what should I do?

*   *   *

1. What are Bill's obligations to the company?

2. What are Bill's obligations to Jim?

3. What are the pressures upon Bill?

4. If Bill wishes to disclose the facts, how extensive should the audience be — his superiors, his department, any other department, the public, a government agency?

5. If his disclosure were to become common knowledge, what would be the impact upon the company?

6. What would be the result if he decided to say nothing?

7. Should you suspect collusion whenever companies quote similar prices?

PART 3

PROBLEMS:
THE ORGANIZATION
IN SOCIETY

7

RELATIONSHIPS WITH OTHER UNITS

Just as the company is influenced by other constituencies in society, those other units are affected by the activities of the company. The role of company officers in this interaction is the subject of the problems dealt with in this chapter. The relationships with its dealers, competitors, labor unions, or other social groupings have a lot to do with the kind of society that emerges in the process. To recognize the requirements to be met in these relationships is one of the significant tasks of the developing executive.

Since many of the primary influences upon the decision-maker in business come from the organization, most of the ethical questions faced in this area tend to be framed with organizational values first in mind. Decisions can be made more readily when policies and procedures are indicated by the firm and are well understood by its members; even when guidelines are not clear, the company comes near the top of the list when close questions of morality come up. It is this not unusual experience in human behavior that has motivated actions to help balance the interests of all parties involved.

The moral positions of a society are potent factors in their own right but often they may be reinforced by legal enactments. Laws intended to prevent excessive control of events by a limited number of individuals have been passed through the years. Without these, we would have to rely on notions of "fair play" to guarantee that people would not be hurt by the indiscriminate exercise of power; but, since this approach has been ineffective all too often, there has been more reliance upon regulation by federal and state laws with agents of government charged with the duty of enforcement.

Another way of accomplishing such a balance involves neither the direct approach of legal sanctions nor the more casual influence of social norms. This method, in which a balance is achieved by letting groups compete for resources, has come to be called *pluralism.* One of the prominent features of American society and its political philosophy, pluralism has come to be an attribute favored by the proponents of *laissez-faire.* They have even pointed to it as a "natural" phenomenon which should be allowed to grow without government regulations to curb it. When Adam Smith wrote of the "invisible hand" of the marketplace, he was testifying to his belief in the inevitability of things taking their course in this fashion.

In practice, pluralism has a rough time of it because of the disparity in power between groups in our society; it is often as ineffective as that other informal mechanism, the weight of social consciousness in the norms of fair play. Consumers may outnumber manufacturers but, even with recent attempts at organized efforts on their behalf, they possess very little of the power available to those with concerted and long-standing activities in their area of expertise. Small firms seldom come off well in direct competition with larger firms, and dealers may find it difficult to challenge the one-sidedness of their relationships with the company whose products they sell.

However, even the eventual return to legal regulation does not provide a fully satisfactory answer, inasmuch as the groups with economic power undoubtedly possess political power as well. An efficient corps of lobbyists can prevent most serious challenges to the comfortable status quo of the economically favored.

In this chapter the reader will need to go beyond the obvious fact of competing constituencies and determine whether proposed efforts toward solving problems are likely to have any practical outcomes. As always, some obvious and direct approaches may prove to be costly. Nor will such a simple response as passing a law to cover the situation necessarily be effective; implementation of a rule often leaves much to be desired, in formal situations as well as in less formal ones.

In most of these problem situations, too, there are usually more individuals and groups concerned than those on the two sides of a case or controversy. Third parties may not be directly involved, but frequently their welfare will be based upon the outcome of deliberations or negotiations between the original two parties. Those indirectly affected may be a small group on the sidelines or they may be as broad a constituency as the citizens of an entire nation.

The Products Engineering Laboratory of the Expro Corporation was faced with several problems in the development of an air pollution control system of great promise. The significant problem was in the high-energy venturi scrubber unit.

Larry Dean, the Laboratory Director, suggested to Dave Roberts, his Senior Researcher, that they turn to at least two outside vendors who were active in the development of air movement systems: "They have the expertise to help us. Alone, we could be working on this for years. And we can get it for no cash outlay on our part."

"What will the outside firms get out of it?" asked Roberts.

"They can hope that if we complete the research successfully, we'll use them as the supplier of materials," Dean opined.

Thus two companies, Alpha Motors, Inc., and Beta Engine Co., participated in the product research and development stage. There was no contract of any kind signed nor was there any express promise made.

The research completed, Expro called for bids for the material. Alpha came in with the lowest bid. Roberts suggested acceptance of the bid, especially since Alpha had also contributed more to the development.

"Beta should get the bid. Write a memo justifying the action on the basis of knowledge of the firm and better service potential," concluded Dean.

*   *   *

1. What might Dave Roberts do now?
2. What responsibilities to the company do both Dean and Roberts have?
3. What responsibility has Expro to either Alpha or Beta?
4. Can Alpha or Beta avoid being placed in a similar position again? How?

Dr. David Donald was the senior researcher on the Caldo Corporation team that developed an important new process for the recovery of waste products from smoke stacks at a development cost of $20 million.

Shortly after, Dr. Donald accepted a position with Freddo, Inc., a competitor of Caldo, to work on their pollution control projects.

In response, Caldo Corp. lawyers sought an injunction to prohibit Donald from accepting the job. The court permitted Donald to accept his new position but restrained him from divulging any of the "trade secrets" accumulated through work on the previous Caldo project.

Donald sought the advice of Freddo lawyers: "What can I say or do? What are trade secrets?"

"We're not sure," replied the lawyers. "We'll have to have another court decision to find out."

Donald was glum. "I want to stay out of trouble but I can't see how."

* * *

1. What can Freddo expect from Dr. Donald in the future?
2. What are Freddo's rights and responsibilities in this matter?
3. Suppose Freddo stepped up its recruiting of key people in the industry even though it had no research program or experience in the field. Would this have been unethical?
4. Whose property is the knowledge of Dr. Donald — his or Caldo's?
5. What were Donald's responsibilities to Caldo?
6. What are Donald's responsibilities to Freddo?

Phil O'Reilly was visibly tired when he got home after a meeting of the union negotiating committee of which he was a member. As president of Local #150 of the United Zirconium Workers of America, he had been playing a significant role in negotiations for a new contract.

"The company is really sticking to its original offer," Phil told his wife Mary, "just like they said they would. Actually it's a lot more than we expected they would give and where we thought we'd end up."

"Why not settle?" asked Mary.

"We should because a strike won't do us any good this year. The only trouble is that headquarters told us to fight on this one, for some reason."

*   *   *

1. What are O'Reilly's responsibilities in this instance and to whom?

2. What are the responsibilities of the national officers of the union?

3. Might the national officers have valid reasons for their stand? What might they be?

4. If they do not, what might be the motivating factors on the part of union officers in these circumstances?

5. The presentation by a company of an offer it believes is fair, rather than starting negotiations at a low figure, has become known as "Boulwarism" (from Lemuel Boulware, who started this policy for General Electric). Why might a company use this approach?

6. How does Boulwarism affect the company, the union, or the community?

The Megaton Steel Company, Inc., one of the country's larger producers, recognized the advantages of establishing production facilities in "America's Heartland." After a careful search the company selected a site in the midst of cornfields not far from the Mississippi River. Although the plant was being located in a sparsely settled area, there were several small industrial cities nearby to provide managerial and clerical talent as well as skilled workers. This was a critical factor since other Megaton plants could not spare scarce personnel and, what is more, few of its people cared to leave their settled urban surroundings to relocate "in the sticks."

The company recruiters mounted a strong campaign in the towns surrounding the plant. They were able to offer salaries and wages that were closer to the rates prevailing at the eastern plants of Megaton than to the local ones. The recruiting accentuated an already "tight" labor situation and gave rise to complaints from existing firms

*   *   *

1. What are some of the advantages in locating where Megaton did?

2. What are the company's responsibilities in this situation? To whom?

3. How might the company support its actions?

4. What could be the results of these actions if the local companies are suppliers for Megaton?

5. What could be the results if the local companies are Megaton's customers?

The Director of Industrial Relations and his staff of the Alpha Zirconium Co. had just emerged from a week of sporadic bargaining when the contract deadline arrived and a strike was called by the leaders of the United Zirconium Workers of America, the union representing the employees.

Talks continued in the same desultory fashion for two weeks until, after one twelve-hour session, the company gave in to the union demands.

In Kelley's Korner Saloon near the mill, a favorite hangout of AZ employees, there was cause for merriment. The crowd included Edgar Thompson, the Assistant Director of Industrial Relations for the company, and Mel Blank, one of the junior members of the union team. As the night progressed and each treated the other to further refreshment, the conviviality increased.

"We really fought for and got our just demands," said Mel with less than sober conviction.

"You've got a lot to learn, boy," replied Thompson. "This package was set up long ago; we knew what the agreement would be."

*   *   *

1. The "sweetheart contract" is an arrangement entered into between union leaders and the employer in the interests of each of those parties. Is this a sweetheart contract?

2. If it is a sweetheart contract, who is affected by it and how?

3. What is Mel Blank's responsibility in this matter?

4. What would happen as the result of Blank's fulfilling what you believe to be his responsibility?

The Magna Corporation attributed its considerable success in great part to its careful selection and placement of dealerships. Its contracts with its dealers were very carefully drawn to allow Magna to scrutinize and review dealers' operations and, in the event of deficiencies in service to the public, to revoke franchises with little difficulty.

Some concern was expressed over these circumstances in Congressional hearings. In defense of Magna's policies and procedures, the Secretary of the Corporation stated: "Our decisions are made not on whim but after careful deliberation. We want the name Magna to be synonomous with quality. We will not stand by idly while customers receive shoddy treatment. They have a right to expect the best service from our dealers and we won't keep those dealers who do not run efficient operations."

*　　*　　*

1. Who is affected by the relationships in this case and to what extent?

2. What are the concerns of the corporation?

3. How might the concerns of the corporation be ordered in a hierarchy? What system might be used to guarantee that each element will be given its proper weight?

4. Suppose the dealer really is opposing an attempt by the corporation to sell a full line of its products, many of which the dealer does not want. Should the dealer prevail?

5. What if the corporation wants to cut down dealers' sales to discounters? Who would be affected by this and how?

6. Suppose the company wants a dealer to agree not to buy from competitors. What are the economic results if such an agreement were to be permitted?

8

RELATIONSHIPS WITH CONSUMERS

No businessman of today (or yesterday, or tomorrow) can ignore the role played by consumers in his operations. What has not always been in the forefront, however, has been the awareness of responsibilities owed by the businessman to this class of individuals. The relationships between economic units and consumers contain a great disparity in position and, therefore, in the power to accomplish important ends in social existence. Up to now, balance has been difficult to achieve and may remain so for the near future.

This chapter continues our consideration of the problems faced in the previous chapter, but it puts into finer focus some of the most pertinent issues faced by the businessman in what may be the most important set of relationships in which he is involved — his dealings with the buyers of his goods and services. Again, the conclusions to be reached depend not so much upon what must be accomplished but upon how it can be done. Dysfunctional consequences are as probable here as in earlier problem cases. What may be sought as a solution to a social evil may bring about conditions that disrupt society even more than the original situations did; making the cure worse than the disease has been a long-standing problem with legislators or social activists who push the panic button in response to an upsetting set of circumstances.

Perhaps the most widespread dilemma is that faced by makers of social policy when, to protect one class of citizens (in this case, the consumer), they place upon economic activity restrictions that may redound to the detriment of others, and may eventually adversely affect even the individuals whom the legislation was intended to protect. The question becomes one of assessing the benefits to be gained in a situation in which protection of the consumer could involve greater costs to him in the long run. It must be realized, however, that this is a facile argument which may be used in an attempt to avoid any regulation whatever; manufacturers may be all too eager to employ this line of reasoning, whether there is much basis for it or not in a given case.

In an earlier era the drive to industrialize and its accompanying values protected industrial activity. Up to now the balance has been weighted in favor of the producer and, to a lesser extent, the seller of goods. The Latin maxim *caveat emptor,* let the buyer beware, is now being replaced by its opposite, *caveat venditor.* The consumer may not be king, but he now has enough in the way of representation to make the seller beware.

A more difficult problem arises when the direct interests of consumers conflict with agreements made in industry. In such a case, one must balance the short-term benefits to consumers against the long-term but more abstract benefits of living up to one's word. For example, in many states dealers can be made to adhere to contracts made with manufacturers to sell products at established price levels ("fair trade") despite obvious savings to consumers if the products could be sold at reduced prices. Is this problem in business ethics a matter of priorities? If so, whose interests come first? Remember that Bentham and the Utilitarians (see Chapter 2) indicated that the highest ethical goal was to provide the maximum amount of happiness for all beings; how this could be accomplished was not entirely clear, but this did not stop Bentham from proposing much social welfare legislation as an active expression of his basic philosophy. Undoubtedly more such practical activity is called for now.

Justin Nichols was an experienced department manager in the men's clothing department for the local store of the W. C. Fields Co.

One day Bob Michaels, a management trainee assigned to Nichols' department, noted that an entire lot of slacks was marked up inadvertently at over a dollar more than the correct price. When Bob called this to Nichols' attention he was told that the mistake would have to stand as is. Bob later found out that many such "mistakes" occurred. Stockroom girls were often asked to markup merchandise to compensate for later markdowns in price or the manager's original errors in judgment in buying. For this the girls received substantial reductions in price on any merchandise they wanted. Bob found further that every manager followed such practices (against store policy), because if he did not, the quarterly results often reflected unfavorably upon him.

When Bob's tour of duty in men's clothing came to an end he was interviewed by the store manager: "Bob, let me know what you've learned here. Be frank. If there's anything I want, it's the truth."

*　　*　　*

1. How much should Bob disclose?

2. Is the store manager likely to be unaware of the actual situation?

3. If Bob discloses all and stays with the firm, what will be the reaction to him of others in the organization?

4. Who is hurt by these techniques — the stock girls, the managers, the trainees, anyone?

5. If he finds out about it, what should the store manager do about the practice?

6. When Bob gets to be a manager what should he do about this type of practice?

Sunnyside Hospital enjoyed the reputation of being a well run institution with above average levels of professional care. Most of the credit for this was given to the Administrator, who was widely praised for his efficiency in operating the facilities. One of the employees who knew how the Administrator accomplished his "miracle" was Will Wright, the chief accountant. Various procedures were used to alter the actual expenses. Among them was the fact that average costs were kept high for the paying patients so that higher costs could be justified for the majority of patients supported by welfare agencies. Often doctors could be encouraged to keep paying patients an extra day. In addition, citizens who contributed their time were paid by check, later endorsed by them back to the hospital, and their labor cost was added to hospital costs.

Will Wright was getting increasingly distraught about the situation, and one day his wife Lil mentioned all this to her friend, Gladys Smith, the wife of the chairman of the hospital board of trustees.

Gladys replied: "For heaven's sake, keep quiet, Lil. The hospital is doing a service to the community. And there's a government grant in the offing. Do you want to spoil everything?"

* * *

1. What is the impact of the procedures employed by the administrator?

2. Which constituencies are most affected by the results?

3. Are there any ways in which the Wrights could justify a disclosure of these circumstances?

4. What would be the results if the Wrights did disclose the situation and it became common knowledge in the community?

5. Of these possible results, which would the Wrights want to bring about by the disclosure? How could they be certain that only the desirable results would follow disclosure?

The Kozy Home Heating Co. operated a thriving furnace inspection-repair-replacement business in Central City.

Sam Jones, the owner of a modest home, was the recipient of seemingly bad news after an inspection of the Jones' furnace by a Kozy representative.

"Mr. Jones, this furnace is dangerous. It could blow up or cause a fire. I can't let you take that chance so I won't put the heating unit back in."

"But it's cold outside," sputtered Jones.

"Well, I'll try hard, seeing it's an emergency, to get a crew here to install a new unit at $1500," replied the representative.

"But I can't afford that," said Jones woefully.

"Don't worry, it will cost you only pennies a day to pay off the bill over three years. We can wait. Sign here," said the Kozy man.

The installation proceeded immediately but the new unit, from the very start, did not function at even the same level as the old one. Despite repeated requests to Kozy to do a proper job, nothing happened.

Two months later an assistant vice president of the First National Bank of Central City called the Jones' home: "Mr. Jones, you are in arrears on the payments on your new furnace. Please begin to make payment or we shall have to take legal action."

Somewhat indignant by this time, Jones stormed: "Those crooks took out a perfectly good furnace and left me with a lousy one. I'm not paying a cent until the work is done. Besides, how did you people get in on this?"

The assistant vice president explained that the paper was discounted by Kozy to the Bank and Jones was legally liable for the amount regardless of what Kozy had or had not done on the furnace.

*   *   *

1. The bank is in the position of being a "holder in due course." This means, essentially, that it is owed the money without the debtor being able to maintain a defense against it in court. Why would a society support this position?

2. If you disagree with the holder in due course doctrine, can you provide alternative approaches in solving the problems it is intended to solve.

3. Is there anything Sam Jones can do at the present time?

4. What alternatives are open to the bank?
5. Outline the possible results of the bank's pursuit of each alternative.

Happy Pappy Stores grew rapidly in the Southwest in the last few years through an imaginative promotional program combined with a sharply competitive pricing policy. One of its recent successful promotions was the use of a heavily advertised "loss leader," *Superhet* radios, which have enjoyed a favorable reputation and a strong sales pattern nationally. When they were advertised by Happy Pappy at a price 40 percent lower than usual there was a decided surge of customers to the stores of the chain.

Not everyone was happy with the results. Mark Updike, the marketing manager for Superhet, got on the telephone to Ben Good, the president of Happy Pappy:

"Mr. Good, you can't sell our radios for that ridiculous price. It's a violation of the fair trade law in your state. Stop it."

This stand did not entirely surprise Good but he had gone ahead with the promotion because he felt strongly about it on grounds of principle.

"Mr. Updike, I've always felt that this kind of price fixing was unfair and a violation of the spirit of free enterprise."

*   *   *

1. What is a "loss leader"? Is it ethical?
2. Fair trade laws in many states represent attempts to support retail prices. What are some effects of such programs?
3. Does Superhet have any justification for being concerned?
4. What can Updike do in this situation?
5. What would be the possible results of his following any of the courses you mentioned in answering question 4?
6. Does anyone else enter into the picture?
7. Are there any grounds other than principle for Ben Good's action?

At Carson, Parson, and Spott, one of the more successful advertising agencies headquartered in New York, Bob Kunkle, the executive vice president, had just called in Jim Graham, the account executive in charge of the account for *Zippy*, a new soft drink made by Papco, Inc. The following exchange of ideas took place.

"Jim, do you have the ad presentation ready for the *Zippy* account? Papco is one of our best clients and I want to go all out on this."

"Right, chief. I'll zip through all the multi-media presentations we've generated to see if they come down the reentry path without burning up."

"Save the Madison Avenue talk for the client, Graham, and get on with it."

"Yes, sir. Well, the basic theme underlying all our ads is that a new ingredient in *Zippy*, hexaminosucrynol, gives you a greater lift sooner and keeps you going the rest of the day."

"Does it?"

"I guess so; at least that's what the Papco people tell me. If it doesn't do anything physiologically at least there can be a psychological lift because people will think so after our ads have emphasized it."

"Does that hexa-whatever-it-is actually promote quicker absorption in the blood stream?"

"Well, chief, what do you want me to do — set up a complete lab and test out all these claims? The Papco boys say it does and I'm not going to call them liars. We need this account."

*   *   *

1. How much responsibility does the ad agency have for checking the accuracy of clients' claims?

2. What is owed to the customer in this situation?

3. What pressures exist on the ad agency, the company, the consumer?

4. How can an ad agency justify a campaign that is not completely accurate? Does it matter whether an agency knows with certainty that the claim is not accurate?

5. Who bears the greater responsibility for the advertised claims about a product — the agency or the company?
6. Critics of advertising say it is wasteful. What could a defense be?

"Groovy" Grover of WQUD was the most popular disc jockey in Central City, and advertising time was easy to sell for his program. Adam Smith, the station manager, was well aware of the contributions to profits made by the "Groovy Show."

One of the heaviest advertisers and largest sources of revenue for WQUD was "Good Deal Charlie," a local agency for Crudleigh V-8's. "Groovy" plugged the auto agency by emphasizing "Quality, integrity, and the lowest prices in town."

Eventually complaints started filtering into Smith's office concerning the customer practices of Good Deal Charlie's sales force. Invariably when customers tried to close a deal on an "irresistible" price (lowest in town) the salesman either found a "math error," added federal excise taxes, or stated that the agency manager "threw me out of the office for going below cost."

Smith approached "Groovy" with this series of complaints and asked for his opinion about a course of action.

"Aw, don't get excited, chief; all these auto dealers say the same thing about service. As far as price goes, all I know is that they gave me a good deal."

* * *

1. Is Groovy's experience a good guide for the station manager's decision?

2. What is the extent of responsibility of the station manager?

3. Does Groovy have any responsibilities in this situation?

4. How common are these practices of auto salesmen? Does that matter?

5. Who is likely to attract potential buyers — Charlie or his competitors?

6. What are the possible alternate sales techniques?

7. What are the possible ways of changing objectionable sales techniques?

Micro Auto Parts, Inc., is a supplier of a wide range of components to the automobile industry. This is a highly competitive segment of the industry and the changes in demand call for careful planning and control of production and pricing on the part of suppliers.

The gloom was thick in the president's office when Frank Singleton, the Vice President of Control Systems, outlined his evaluation of the situation:

"We have so many fixed costs now that staying in business will take some doing."

"Right, but things are tough all over the industry," responded the president.

"That's exactly why we should make that very low bid I suggested on the brake systems for U.S. Motors. None of the other suppliers would come close."

"But there wouldn't be any profit in it, and we might even lose money," said the president with the last word.

* . * *

1. What might be the effect of a low bid upon the buyers?

2. How might competitors react?

3. What are the implications for the ultimate consumers?

4. Suppose a new process would produce a better system with a profit, despite a 40 percent price cut. Who would benefit and in what way?

5. What might be the ultimate result in the industry of the situation described in question 4?

Kallahan's Department Store long enjoyed the largest volume of any merchandiser in Central City. The owners of the parent company were concerned, however, with the low return on their investment. They sent Jameson Jones to take over the Central City store in the hope that he could turn things around.

One of the first points of departure for Jones was to seek ways of reducing operational costs:

"Look at our merchandise return figures — they're horrible," said Jones. "From now on we take no returned merchandise that doesn't have a sales tag attached, even if they come off easily. Also, instead of customer service desks on all floors, we will have only one return desk on the twelfth floor with one clerk, Albert Sourwine, in charge."

"But J.J.," remarked his assistant, "people will have trouble finding the place. Also, Sourwine gets pretty cranky — he's not the public relations type."

*   *   *

1. What are the probable results of the moves proposed by Jones?

2. Is it likely that Jones knows the consequences of his actions?

3. Can Jones justify his techniques? How?

4. What are the duties owed the customers by the store?

5. Suppose the store insists upon its legal rights in each instance. What results are likely?

6. Do customers have any responsibilities in this matter?

José Garcia, his wife, and two children under six years of age recently arrived in Magnolia City from Puerto Rico. More fortunate than many, the family found housing and José obtained work. His wages, however, barely covered the rent and food bills, leaving little for clothing or other expenses.

A month after their arrival the Garcia family was visited by Manuel Zorro, a Spanish-speaking salesman for the *Exceptional Encyclopedia*.

"You can see how America is the land of opportunity but only for those with an education. Your children will be handicapped unless they can keep up with the other children. This set of books will do that."

"We want the best for our children but we have little money," replied José.

"Never fear. We want to take care of our people. Sign this paper and we will let you pay only a few pennies a day. For the cost of a package of cigarettes each day your children will be educated."

José and his wife signed the installment contract to purchase a set of the encyclopedia for $1,165.00 plus interest charges over three years.

*   *   *

1. Can you defend a sale like this?
2. If you are concerned, what remedies do you suggest?
3. Outline the possible results of the remedies suggested?
4. What is the impact of such activities upon the community at large?

9

THE COMMUNITY

The societal nature of the business firm is not open to question. As one of the most effective providers of goods, it satisfies not only those material needs but other, more intangible ones as well. The power the economic organization commands is a source of anxiety to some but, by the same token, its very ability to control represents a strong potential for active and productive efforts toward solving basic problems facing that society.

The fundamental question in this area may well be whether the corporation should be the conscience of the larger collectivity of which it is a part. Inasmuch as a corporation is a "person" in the eyes of the law, it could be viewed as having many of the same social duties with respect to the community as natural persons do, or perhaps even more, since corporations are more powerful persons than ordinary mortals are.

Some resistance exists to the notion that corporations should be active in this manner; much of the opposition rests on practical grounds as well as on philosophical bases. One legal position is that the assets of the corporation belong to the stockholders and therefore cannot be distributed in ventures outside the corporation's main area of activity. The response is that being a good citizen of the community is part of the activity of a corporation and that contributions to the welfare of the immediate society are expected as part of this responsibility. Even assuming that this orientation to community giving is a legitimate part of the role of the corporation (and most executives would agree that this is the case), additional questions arise as to extent of the support required. Who gets the money and how much is a practical question, the answers to which reflect a set of value judgments or determinations of social policy on the part of the corporation. This is nothing new, of course, for individuals and organizations have been contributing to charities for a long time. In previous eras, however, the giving of money was a personal matter with the philanthropist who owned the company. Few of these are left, and today's executive manages the assets for the real owners, the stockholders, without having much in the way of ownership himself. Again, the problem may resolve itself into a matter of priorities; which of the constituencies comes first?

An even more difficult aspect of the same basic problem lies in the participation of the corporation in the community along other than financial paths. The question of the extent to which the corporation should be active in its milieu by being the "conscience of the community" has been identified as a matter of current concern. Earlier entrepreneurs often saw themselves as "community con-sciences" to the extent that they prescribed the conditions of the private conduct of their employees; apparently Henry Ford even visited the homes of his workers to determine if they were leading "decent" lives. Such heavy-handed paternalism is virtually absent in this day and age, even though some subtle influences of this kind remain in the unwritten corporation codes of dress, residence, and style of life. Our present concerns for the quality of individual and group life may have made us more resistant to these social demands than were our forefathers.

Earlier chapters of this book raised the problems of direct pressures upon the individual; in this chapter, though cast in another form, those same questions about individual autonomy and existence reappear. Here the problems put into focus the impact of the corporation upon the lives of collected individuals. Should a corporate citizen, with all the power available to it, impose its own values upon other citizens? If we are concerned about control, we can answer readily in the negative; others respond that the corporation already has tried to impose its own economic and social values by "selling free enterprise," and that it should now play a broader role in society by encouraging others in the community to foster social or civil rights and responsibilities. The question resolves itself to one necessitating a decision as to what set of values or whose moral standards are to be pursued.

The problems in this area are made all the more complicated by the fact that a corporation is not a monolithic actor with all elements in it moving in one unified effort. It is, as most readers recognize, a highly complex, dynamic system of interacting personalities. Because each individual has his own set of motivating values, it is naive to believe that any organization moves as one physical body in single-minded fashion. Analysts of organizational decision-making must, therefore, keep in mind the varied and often conflicting goals and dynamisms of the individuals in that organization.

Sweetco is a distributor of candy and cigarettes in a wide geographic area around the small, quiet county seat of Chummy Falls. Recent news media coverage of violence and disrespect for the law had aroused strong reactions among the townsfolk of Chummy Falls. Sweetco, as the leading business entity in town, was, through its employees, an active participant in programs designed to eliminate crime and juvenile delinquency.

One quiet summer day Chuck Grimstad, a driver-deliveryman for Sweetco, started to make a delivery to a news stand across the street from the First National Bank. Suddenly, Chuck heard a cry for help. It seemed to come from the direction of the bank, but he couldn't be sure. All he saw was a man hurrying in a furtive manner and carrying a bulging shopping bag toward a waiting car. Chuck paused, worrying about what he should do, especially since the company had a rule that drivers were not to leave their open trucks. Then, deciding suddenly to investigate, he ran past the bank to chase the man with the shopping bag. As he passed the alley next to the bank he noticed some youths engaged in horseplay. At this point other bystanders came up, attracted by the same shouts; it became obvious that there was nothing wrong in the bank and that the shouts for help came from the young pranksters.

Unfortunately, in all the excitement, someone drove off with the Sweetco truck and its contents. When it was later found empty the company calculated that the loss was significant enough to cause them to consider some employment cutbacks in the present slow season.

The Personnel Manager, the Vice President of Marketing, and the Dispatcher met the next day to determine what to do. Grimstad had clearly violated a basic company rule that an open truck was not to be left unattended under any circumstances.

In his defense Chuck stated: "But all I did was act like a good citizen should. You can't blame me for that."

*   *   *

1. What would be the reasons for punishing Grimstad for his violation of the company rule.

2. Is there any reason for ignoring the rule violation in this case?

3. If no publicity is given to the rule violation, would this help?

4. Suppose the company disciplined Grimstad and then discovered that he was selected "Good Citizen of the Week." What position should company officers take?

J.B. Bragdon, the Executive Vice President of Wispro, was widely regarded throughout the company for his keen awareness of the personal and social requisites for success in the company. When "J.B." made a comment it was usually considered seriously by those to whom it was directed. One day over lunch in the executive dining room J.B. remarked to Chauncey Walsingham, the Director of Marketing and a somewhat younger man than J.B., that he ought to consider joining the Forsythia Club, the most exclusive social club in Central City, where the company had its headquarters. "Be glad to put your name up for membership, boy; just give me the word," said J.B.

Chauncey pondered this a bit and rejoined, "But, J.B., isn't the Forsythia Club restricted?"

"What do you mean, restricted?" puffed J.B. "If you mean we select the people we want to associate with, and meet a bunch of important people every day — yes, we are restricted."

"No, I mean aren't Jews and Negroes excluded from membership?" replied Chauncey.

Upon confirmation of this point, Chauncey opined that he might have serious reservations about belonging to a club with such restrictions. "Don't be silly, boy. You know how valuable it would be to you to belong," replied J.B. with an air of finality.

*   *   *

1. What is J. B. referring to when he mentions the alleged values in belonging?

2. Assuming there is such value to the company in a club membership, are there any other considerations to be faced?

3. Can you weigh any possible competing considerations? Which might outweigh the others?

4. Are some factors more immediate than others? Which?

5. Assume Chauncey becomes a member of the club and continues to disagree with the membership restrictions. What do you think he should do about it?

6. What are the probable outcomes of each course of action?

7. What would be the effect of each approach upon Chauncey's future with the company?

Southern Coke and Carbon is a steel producing subsidiary of the American Steel Corporation (ASC) and is located in Magnolia City, one of the South's largest industrial cities. Southern Coke is the largest employer in the community. Activist groups in Magnolia City were early in the forefront of efforts to promote racial equality in industry and in the community generally.

At this time, Sam Sims, a top reporter from the *Northeastern Beacon,* interviewed Ronald A. Morgan, the president of the subsidiary. The interview included the following exchange:

"Mr. Morgan, there has been an indication of strong barriers against the employment and promotion of Negroes in your plant here in the city."

"Mr. Sims, if the Union has discriminatory policies and if individuals in the community also discriminate on a racial basis, there is not much we can do. Our company policy is to promote equal opportunity. We'll always try to do what is right, but we can't go around telling others what to do."

Publication of this information in the Sunday issue of the *Beacon* aroused a lot of comment in the community. Enough was generated pro and con to cause the issuance of a statement from the headquarters of ASC (located in a large Northern city). The statement indicated the concern of ASC with the problem and its intention to persuade others in a resonable manner to be tolerant.

*   *   *

1. Is the company a significant social entity in the community?
2. What duties are owed by Southern Coke and Carbon to the community?
3. What are the probable results of company inaction in this area?
4. What are the probable results of positive action?
5. Should Morgan have adopted a different position?
6. What might headquarters have done differently? With what results?
7. What are some of the possible impacts upon the company's various constituencies of the statement from headquarters? The statement in the paper?

8. What are some of the pressures that might have been brought to bear upon SCC and ASC?

The headquarters of the Caldo Corporation was in a heightened state of excitement. Not only was the annual stockholders meeting only two weeks away, but, in addition, the radical activist group named "Stop the War in the Near East" announced its intentions to demonstrate at the meeting and, presumably, to disrupt it. The primary concern of the group was with the manufacture by the corporation of *Caldo-Crisp*, an incendiary device with some tatical use in warfare.

This morning, W.W. Braham, the visibly distraught president of Caldo, rushed into the office of his executive vice president, Charles Bedford.

"Chuck, what in blazes is going on at your alma mater, Ivy College? The Board of Trustees has been asked by these radicals to give proxies on the block of shares the College holds so that those grimy guys can elect some directors to our board. They're trying that with all the colleges that hold our stock."

"Wow, W.W.! What can we do to nip this in the bud? I could get on the phone to the president of Ivy. Our graduates in the company have always been good for big contributions to the alumni fund. We ought to tell them where to go when they come around asking for money this year. Ivy needs our support to keep going and they're not going to get it if they decide to give their proxies to that bunch."

*   *   *

1. In what ways do companies support colleges?

2. Is pressure on an educational institution justified? How?

3. How extensive is the proxy problem of Caldo (or similar corporations)?

4. What alternatives does Caldo have in meeting its problems with proxies?

5. If Caldo-Crisp represents only 2 percent of its sales volume, does pointing to this fact represent a good answer by the company to its critics.

6. What obligations does the company have toward the dissenters?

7. What other constituencies are involved? What are the company's responsibilities to each?

8. Are some of these responsibilities in conflict with each other?
9. What is Ivy's position in this situation? How should it react?

Rumors of an impending move of the main plant of the Fugo Corporation out of Oxygen Falls to a new site far away had been standard fare in the town for many years. It was understandable that such rumors should circulate because it was fairly common knowledge that the plant facilities were in need of updating. Any such move would have dire consequences for the town since Fugo, with 2,000 employees, was the largest employer and the main prop of the local economy.

This time the rumor included the specific information that a rural Midwestern site had been selected and that a plant would be ready there within a year. This prompted Sam Bean, the mayor of the town, to rush to W. E. Knough, the plant manager, to find out whether Fugo really intended to move and, if so, to urge the plant manager to intercede at headquarters to stop the move.

Another visitor at Knough's office was Frank Webb, a capable young engineer who had contributed significantly to the success of many company projects. Frank told the manager: "W.E., I've been hearing these rumors about a plant move, and I need to know whether there's any truth to them. I can't move from here; my wife won't do it, and I also have a sick brother to look after. I've just been offered a pretty good job with the State Highway Department. Naturally I want to continue here, but I have to say yes or no on the job offer within a week."

Mr. Knough got on the phone to company headquarters — not to find out about the move (he already knew), but to find out how he should react. "Don't say a thing about it," the company president cautioned. "You know what kind of trouble you'll have if you do. Wait until the shutdown in ten months."

*   *   *

1. What kind of trouble does the company president have in mind?
2. How might this trouble be avoided or dampened?
3. What responsibility has Knough to Frank Webb? To the other employees?
4. What responsibility has Knough to his company?
5. What responsibilities has the company to the community?

6. If Sam Bean, the mayor, were a high plant official with advance knowledge, what would his responsibilities be — to the town, to the company?

7. Does the president have a right to require complete secrecy on the part of his staff in the town?

The Omni Corporation was long accustomed to playing an active role in housing decisions of its managerial personnel. The company would help in the buying and selling of houses of moving executives in order to prevent any financial losses upon transfer.

As the result of demands that the blue-collar ranks be included in this program, the Company Real Estate Office (REO) began to help other employees with their realty transfers. The sheer number of blue-collar employees, however, limited the role of the office to advice and maintenance of a small list of realtors who were active in the market. A majority of these brokers specialized in modestly priced properties, many of which were located in "changing neighborhoods."

In this hot summer it came to the attention of Ted White, the REO manager, that one of the realtors, Sam Smith, was contacting a large number of Omni employees and offering to sell their houses before property values declined further.

White checked with some of the Smith clients; to a man they were grateful to Smith for what they considered good advice. On the other hand, the local *Save Our Neighborhood Association* called with complaints about the practice.

White wondered what he should do.

*   *   *

1. What realtor Smith is doing here is called "blockbusting." What is the impact upon the community of this practice?
2. What are the various constituencies affected by the company's policy?
3. Is there any ordering of priorities among the constituencies?
4. What should basic company policy be in these circumstances?
5. What should the realtor do under these conditions?
6. What role can Ted White play?
7. What happens if the corporation eliminates its real estate services?

10

THE ENVIRONMENT

The quality of life, both in a physical and psychological frame of reference, generates many of our current questions and concerns and activates the latent stirrings for social service that for many were dormant in recent years. Agreement here, as with all preceding areas under consideration, is easy to attain; what is not simple is the recognition of how this agreement on principles may be translated into action, given the competing interests and the complexity of the conditions.

The solutions to most of the problems raised in this chapter are technically feasible; the primary question is one of cost — how much and who pays? Few people will dispute the continuing need for clear air and clean water, but when the bill is presented, most fumble to let the other guy pay. Moral obligations in this connection are sketchily drawn, and even legal requirements are not clear. In this case individuals and groups often fall back on the simple expedient of passing on the costs to others — thus adding another moral dimension to the problem. As economic institutions have many constituencies to keep in mind — stockholders, employees, consumers, and the general public — the large number of persons affected by any economic decision makes the resulting cost distribution even more critical. As in earlier chapters, the matter of priorities is the essence of the problem facing the decision-maker.

Additional complications come from the greater number of ramifications of a corporate decision in this area, as compared with a decision by a private individual or a government agency. Certain steps can be taken to improve the environment around polluting industrial plants, but if the cost cannot be absorbed by the company it must close its doors. The impact upon jobs is direct, as some communities have recognized at various stages of development. Some plants have been lured to communities where the citizens recognized the pollution possibilities but have opted for the jobs to be made available; the tradeoffs involved have been recognized. At the same time it must be stated that some executives have found responses in terms of economic survival serve as a ready excuse for poor administrative or technological practice. A clean environment may be economically feasible after all; the attempt to provide the answer just takes more ability or work than the manager wishes to or can provide.

Some arguments are made for the continuance of questionable practices until it has been demonstrated to the satisfaction of all that these practices may be harmful. The tobacco industry, for instance, continues to believe that smoking is not hazardous and points to increased consumption of cigarettes as an indication that the public generally agrees with that position. How much definitive information is needed before decisions on public health can be made is as much in dispute now as it has been in the past history of scientific discovery.

The complexity of technical questions and the overwhelming amount of data necessary for decisions in this area aggravate the situation. Government agents who are charged with the responsibility for monitoring these activities are often accused of shirking their duties; their major response to the accusations is that they are understaffed and outnumbered by their industrial counterparts. Responses by citizens' groups often suggest that civil servants find it uncomfortable to challenge corporation activities and easier to go along without making trouble. These same citizens' organizations have undoubtedly come into existence because of these strong feelings that government agencies were falling down on the job. Whether these private groups can accomplish much, given their lack of economic power, remains to be seen. It takes a lot of organization of effort to match the capabilities for action possessed by industrial entities.

If we stretch the meaning of the term *pollution,* there is another source of pollution that merits our attention. Recent challenges to preexisting standards of conduct have been thought of in terms such as "mind pollution," with some elements in the community even tying it in with foreign conspiracies to undermine our society. What some see as a departure from hypocrisy in depicting human behavior is viewed by others as a weakening of the moral fiber of the country. What standards can be applied has even the best legal minds in the country in a quandry — and with little wonder, since these questions lie on the difficult area of overlap between law and morality. When the moral sentiments of only a segment of the community are carried through into law, difficulties usually ensue.

In summary, the problems in this final chapter resemble others in earlier chapters but provide the decision-maker with even more difficulty because more people and organizations are involved. The ramifications of these problem situations offer a suitable challenge.

Dewar and Sons, Inc., a small, family-owned company, has leased a valuable seam of coal to a strip-mining concern. This mining company has had extensive strip-mining experience and is one of the most reputable mining firms in the state. The firm is financially sound and possesses a Triple A credit rating.

A sportsmen's organization, Save-Our-Streams (SOS), has been stocking a stream that runs through private property where the fishing is informally restricted to youngsters in the area. In addition, SOS has been treating natural coal seam run-off with limestone to prevent contamination of the stream.

The mining company has secured a strip-mining water permit from the state which allows the drainage from the mine to be channeled into another presently contaminated stream.

The sportsmen's organization is violently opposed to the strip-mining, contending that an accident of any kind may cause the drainage to flow into "its stream," a stream which it neither owns nor received permission to use.

The seam was recently purchased by Dewar for the express purpose of both strip and deep mining of the coal. The amount of coal is extensive and possesses a substantial market value. The president of Dewar is wondering whether to pursue the realization of a just profit from the investment or forego this in favor of an ecological status quo.

*   *   *

1. What is the ecological status quo?
2. How can the company justify a decision to go ahead with the mining?
3. What might the company experience as a result of that decision?
4. What support for its position does SOS have?
5. In whose interests is SOS active?
6. Are there any other alternative courses of action?

Executives of the small textile plant that was the major employer in a small Southern town complained repeatedly to the municipal officials about the lack of water for its operations.

"If we have to struggle along on this little water we can't dilute the waste water from our dyeing operations enough to meet the requirements of the state water pollution code," said the plant superintendent.

"Sorry," said the mayor, "but our tax revenues are not enough to finance any new water towers or lines. You'll just have to make do."

When the company was fined a substantial sum in the following week, it announced that it could no longer continue in business under the present circumstances. Three hundred workers joined the ranks of the unemployed two weeks later.

*   *   *

1. What is the economic impact of the closing upon the town?
2. What were the duties owed by the town officials in this situation?
3. What was the primary duty of the company to the community?
4. What would you have done in the first instance if you were mayor approached by the plant superintendent?
5. What would you do when the company announced it would close? After it had closed?

The Whippet Bus Lines maintain their own terminals throughout the territory they serve. The company leases terminal space to various other firms that provide services to travelers on the Whippet Lines. The largest of these lessees is the Arex Drug Company. The Arex locations sell miscellaneous goods, but the largest volume lies in the sale of newspapers, magazines, and paperbacks.

One fine spring day Liza Dolittle, announcing she was the representative of the League for Clean Literature, demanded to see the Manager of Whippet's Central City terminal, Adam Gray.

"How can you allow this filthy literature in your bus station where all the young passengers have access to it? You must have it removed."

"Madam," replied Gray, "the news stand is run by an independent company that makes its own policy. We can't tell them what to do. I understand, too, that the distributor requires each news stand to take an amount of this material or they won't receive an allotment of the finer magazines and books that you prefer."

"Pornography also pays more in profits," Miss Dolittle responded. "Do something about it or we'll picket your station."

*   *   *

1. Does the League have any basis for its intent to picket?

2. Are there any alternatives the League may pursue?

3. Is Adam Gray's position tenable?

4. What arrangements could be made concerning the relationships between Arex and the distributor?

5. What should the Whippet Bus Lines do?

In testimony seeking a variance from the Pollution Control Board of Appalachia County, Robert Coke, the Manager of Environmental Controls for the main plant of Alpha Steel Company, made a strong statement about the difficulties he faced.

"We don't have the technology right now to handle the problems we have in smoke emission. The levels of control you have to administer are impossible to meet."

Subsequent testimony came from Molly Gates, the president of the Citizens for Cleaner Air: "Mr. Coke used to be the Director of Enforcement for this Board. In that job he cited this very plant he works in for a violation of the smoke control ordinance. Now after he was hired for a high salary by Alpha he's changed his tune. Conditions haven't changed any since then."

Another citizen, John Bell, was of the opinion that the requisite technology was available for handling smoke emission. "Bag-rooms, for instance, have been around for fifty years. Alpha can do it now."

*   *   *

1. What are Coke's responsibilities now?
2. Have they changed from those he had as Director of Enforcement?
3. What are Alpha's responsibilities?
4. Is there anything the pollution Control Board should have done before the situation reached this point?
5. Can Robert Coke say anything in defense of his position?
6. Are there any other points Molly Gates might make?
7. What are some other situations in which the basic features of this problem are likely to be found?
8. What is required of John Bell in this situation?
9. What is Alpha's likely response to Bell?

At a regularly scheduled meeting of the Board of Directors of the Magna Corporation, the chairman accepted a motion to transmit an additional assessment of $300,000 to the Engine Manufacturer's Educational Association, with headquarters in Washington, D.C., in order to aid in the expansion of a public education program and to help the enforcement of an industry code of ethics.

One of the members asked for more details. "I suspect this will mean a special lobbying campaign against further legislation curbing smoke emission from industrial plants. I question whether we should oppose such legislation."

The chairman responded: "We want to educate Congress and the public on the fact that our members are complying with the existing laws. Any further legislation is unnecessary and, if passed, could do serious harm to our nation and its citizens by upsetting the natural course of events. The motion should be passed."

*   *   *

1. Can you support the stand of the chairman?

2. What would passing the motion mean for the stockholders?

3. Opposing the motion would also mean opposing education. Comment on this fact.

4. What is the role of the industry code of ethics?

5. Is lobbying illegal or unethical?

The Marketing Vice President of Papco, Inc., was chairing a strategy meeting for the promotion and distribution of Zippy, their new soft drink.

When it was suggested that the company convert to a new nonreturnable bottle, the staff representative from production objected that these were more expensive and difficult to produce than glass bottles. The marketing staff then reported that their survey indicated a strong preference among consumers for non-returnable bottles.

"Gentlemen," said the Assistant to the President, "we've been deluged with complaints from the Citizens for Pollution Control (CPC) about nonreturnable bottles. They may start boycotting us."

* * *

1. What is the basis for complaints by the Citizens for Pollution Control?

2. What could be some outcomes of a decision to continue using glass containers?

3. Who in the company would agree with the CPC and for what reasons?

4. What should the vice president do?

APPENDIX A

Public Law 88-352 – July 2, 1964

Civil Rights Act of 1964

Title VII – Equal Employment Opportunity

Discrimination Because of Race, Color, Religion, Sex, or National Origin

§ 703. (a) It shall be an unlawful employment practice for an employer –

(1) to fail or refuse to hire or to discharge any individual, or otherwise to discriminate against any individual with respect to his compensation, terms, conditions, or privileges of employment, because of such individual's race, color, religion, sex, or national origin; or

(2) to limit, segregate, or classify his employees in any way which would deprive or tend to deprive any individual of employment opportunities or otherwise adversely affect his status as an employee, because of such individual's race, color, religion, sex, or national origin.

(b) It shall be an unlawful employment practice for an employment agency to fail or refuse to refer for employment, or otherwise to discriminate against, any individual because of his race, color, religion, sex, or national origin, or to classify or refer for employment any individual on the basis of his race, color, religion, sex, or national origin.

(c) It shall be an unlawful employment practice for a labor organization —

(1) to exclude or to expel from its membership, or otherwise to discriminate against, any individual because of his race, color, religion, sex, or national origin;

(2) to limit, segregate, or classify its membership, or to classify or fail or refuse to refer for employment any individual, in any way which would deprive or tend to deprive any individual of employment opportunities, or would limit such employment opportunities or otherwise adversely affect his status as an employee or as an applicant for employment, because of such individual's race, color, religion, sex, or national origin; or

(3) to cause or attempt to cause an employer to discriminate against an individual in violation of this section.

(d) It shall be an unlawful employment practice for any employer, labor organization, or joint labor-management committee controlling apprenticeship or other training or retraining, including on-the-job training programs to discriminate against any individual becuase of his race, color, religion, sex, or national origin in admission to, or employment in, any program established to provide apprenticeship or other training.

(e) Notwithstanding any other provision of this title, (1) it shall not be an unlawful employment practice for an employer to hire and employ employees, for an employment agency to classify, or refer for employment any individual, for a labor organization to classify its membership or to classify or refer for employment any individual, or for an employer, labor organization, or joint labor-management committee controlling apprenticeship or other training or retraining programs to admit or employ any individual in any such program, on the basis of his religion, sex, or national origin in those certain instances where religion, sex, or national origin is a bona fide occupational qualification reasonably necessary to the normal operation of that particular business or enterprise, and (2) it shall not be an unlawful employment practice for a school, college, university, or other educational institution or institution of learning to hire and employ employees of a particular religion if such school, college, university, or other educational institution or institution of learning is, in whole or in substantial part, owned, supported, controlled, or managed by a particular religion or by a particular religious corporation, association, or society, or if the curriculum of such school, college, university, or other educational institution or institution of learning is directed toward the propagation of a particular religion.

(f) As used in this title, the phrase "unlawful employment practice" shall not be deemed to include any action or measure taken by an employer, labor organization, joint labor-management committee, or employment agency with respect to an individual who is a member of the Communist Party of the United States or of any other organization required to register as a Communist-action or Communist-front organization by final order of the Subversive Activities Control Board pursuant to the Subversive Activities Control Act of 1950.

(g) Notwithstanding any other provision of this title, it shall not be an unlawful employment practice for an employer to fail or refuse to hire and employ any individual for any position, for an employer to discharge any individual from any position, or for an employment agency to fail or refuse to refer any individual for employment in any position, or for a labor organization to fail or refuse to refer any individual for employment in any position, if —

(1) the occupancy of such position, or access to the premises in or upon which any part of the duties of such position is performed or is to be performed, is subject to any requirement imposed in the interest of the national security of the United States under any security program in effect pursuant to or administered under any statute of the United States or any Executive order of the President; and

(2) such individual has not fulfilled or has ceased to fulfill that requirement.

(h) Notwithstanding any other provision of this title, it shall not be an unlawful employment practice for an employer to apply different standards of compensation, or different terms, conditions, or privileges of employment pursuant to a bona fide seniority or merit system, or a system which measures earnings by quantity or quality of production or to employees who work in different locations, provided that such differences are not the result of an intention to discriminate because of race, color, religion, sex, or national origin, nor shall it be an unlawful employment practice for an employer to give and to act upon the results of any professionally developed ability test provided that such test, its administration or action upon the results is not designed, intended or used to discriminate because of race, color, religion, sex, or national origin. It shall not be an unlawful employment practice under this title for any employer to differentiate upon the basis of sex in determining the amount of the wages or compensation paid or to be paid to employees of such employer if such differentiation is authorized by the provisions of section 6(d) of the Fair Labor Standards Act of 1938, as amended (29 U.S.C. 206(d)).

(i) Nothing contained in this title shall apply to any business or enterprise on or near an Indian reservation with respect to any publicly announced employment practice of such business or enterprise under which a preferential treatment is given to any individual because he is an Indian living on or near a reservation.

(j) Nothing contained in this title shall be interpreted to require any employer, employment agency, labor organization, or joint labor-management committee subject to this title to grant preferential treatment to any individual or to any group because of the race, color, religion, sex, or national origin of such individual or group on account of an imbalance which may exist with respect to the total number or percentage of persons of any race, color, religion, sex, or national origin employed by any employer, referred or classified for employment by any employment agency or labor organization, admitted to membership or classified by any labor organization, or admitted to, or employed in, any apprenticeship or other training program, in comparison with the total number of percentage of persons of such race, color, religion, sex, or national origin in any community, State, section, or other area, or in the available work force in any community, State, section, or other area.

APPENDIX B

Public Law 90-321 – May 29, 1968
Consumer Credit Protection Act
Title I Consumer Credit Cost Disclosure

§ 101. **Short Title**

This title may be cited as the Truth in Lending Act.

§ 102. **Findings and declaration of purpose**

The Congress finds that economic stabilization would be enhanced and the competition among the various financial institutions and other firms engaged in the extension of consumer credit would be strengthened by the informed use of credit. The informed use of credit results from an awareness of the cost thereof by consumers. It is the purpose of this title to assure a meaningful disclosure of credit terms so that the consumer will be able to compare more readily the various credit terms available to him and avoid the uninformed use of credit. . . .

§ 106. **Determination of finance charge**

(a) Except as otherwise provided in this section, the amount of the finance charge in connection with any consumer credit transaction shall be determined as the sum of all charges, payable directly or indirectly by the person to whom the credit is extended, and imposed directly or indirectly by the creditor as an incident to the extension of credit, including any of the following types of charges which are applicable:

(1) Interest, time price differential, and any amount payable under a point, discount, or other system of additional charges.

(2) Service or carrying charge.

(3) Loan fee, finder's fee, or similar charge.

(4) Fee for an investigation or credit report.

(5) Premium or other charge for any guarantee or insurance protecting the creditor against the obligor's default or other credit loss.

(b) Charges or premiums for credit life, accident, or health insurance written in connection with any consumer credit transaction shall be included in the finance charge unless

(1) the coverage of the debtor by the insurance is not a factor in the approval by the creditor of the extension of credit, and this fact is clearly disclosed in writing to the person applying for or obtaining the extension of credit; and

(2) in order to obtain the insurance in connection with the extension of credit, the person to whom the credit is extended must give specific affirmative written indication of his desire to do so after written disclosure to him of the cost thereof.

(c) Charges or premiums for insurance, written in connection with any consumer credit transaction, against loss of or damage to property or against liability arising out of the ownership or use of property, shall be included in the finance charge unless a clear and specific statement in writing is furnished by the creditor to the person to whom the credit is extended, setting forth the cost of the insurance is obtained from or through the creditor, and stating that the person to whom the credit is extended may choose the person through which the insurance is to be obtained.

(d) If any of the following items is itemized and disclosed in accordance with the regulations of the Board in connection with any transaction, then the creditor need not include that item in the computation of the finance charge with respect to that transaction:

(1) Fees and charges prescribed by law which actually are or will be paid to public officials for determining the existence of or for perfecting or releasing or satisfying any security related to the credit transaction.

(2) The premium payable for any insurance in lieu of perfecting any security interest otherwise required by the creditor in connection with the transaction, if the premium does not exceed the fees and charges described in paragraph (1) which would otherwise be payable.

(3) Taxes.

(4) Any other type of charge which is not for credit and the exclusion of which from the finance charge is approved by the Board by regulation.

§ 107. Determination of annual percentage rate

(a) The annual percentage rate applicable to any extension of consumer credit shall be determined, in accordance with the regulations of the Board,

    (1) in the case of any extension of credit other than under an open end credit plan, as

        (A) that nominal annual percentage rate which will yield a sum equal to the amount of the finance charge when it is applied to the unpaid balances of the amount financed, calculated according to the actuarial method of allocating payments made on a debt between the amount financed and the amount of the finance charge, pursuant to which a payment is applied first to the accumulated finance charge and the balance is applied to the unpaid amount financed; or

        (B) the rate determined by any method prescribed by the Board as a method which materially simplifies computation while retaining reasonable accuracy as compared with the rate determined under subparagraph (A).

    (2) in the case of any extension of credit under an open end credit plan, as the quotient (expressed as a percentage) of the total finance charge for the period to which it relates divided by the amount upon which the finance charge for that period is based, multiplied by the number of such periods in a year.

(b) Where a creditor imposes the same finance charge for balances within a specified range, the annual percentage rate shall be computed on the median balance within the range, except that if the Board determines that a rate so computed would not be meaningful, or would be materially misleading, the annual percentage rate shall be computed on such other basis as the Board may by regulation require.

(c) The annual percentage rate may be rounded to the nearest quarter of 1 per centum for credit transactions payable in substantially equal installments when a creditor determines the total finance charge on the basis of a single add-on, discount, periodic, or other rate, and the rate is converted into an annual percentage rate under procedures prescribed by the Board.

(d) The Board may authorize the use of rate tables or charts which may provide for the disclosure of annual percentage rates which vary from the rate determined in accordance with subsection (a)(1)(A) by not more than such tolerances as the Board may allow. The Board may not allow a tolerance greater than 8 per centum of that rate except to simplify compliance where irregular payments are involved.

(e) In the case of creditors determining the annual precentage rate in a manner other than as described in subsection (c) or (d), the Board may authorize other reasonable tolerances.

(f) Prior to January 1, 1971, any rate required under this title to be disclosed as a percentage rate may, at the option of the creditor, be expressed in the form of the corresponding ratio of dollars per hundred dollars.

APPENDIX C

Allegheny County Health Department
Rules and Regulations

Article XVII — Air Pollution Control

1700. **DECLARATION OF POLICY** It shall be the policy of the County of Allegheny, in cooperation with Federal and State authorities, industry and other interested groups, to achieve and maintain purity of its air resources consistent with the health, welfare and comfort of the residents of the County and the protection of property and resources, and to that end to require the use of all available methods of preventing and controlling air pollution in the County.

1701. **PURPOSE** This Article provides regulations for the control of air pollution within the County of Allegheny; provides definitions; provides for the administration and enforcement of these regulations; provides standards; establishes an Air Pollution Control Advisory Committee; establishes a Board of Air Pollution Appeals and Variance Review; provides for permits, fees, and standards for the installation, construction, addition to, alteration, and use of fuel and refuse burning installations, processes, equipment and devices; provides standards and fees regulating and requiring the installation of smoke abatement, dust arresting, and other air pollution control equipment and monitors; regulates the sale, use and consumption of certain solid fuels; provides for the inspection of all equipment, devices, plants and processes required by this Article; provides for variances, hearings, fines and penalties for violations of this Article; and repeals Article XIII, "Smoke and Air Pollution Control" of the Allegheny County Health Department Rules and Regulations.

F. Board of Air Pollution Appeals and Variance Review

1. The Board of County Commissioners shall appoint a Board of Air Pollution Appeals and Variance Review consisting of five (5) members one (1) of whom shall be designated by the Board of County Commissioners as Chairman and three (3) of whom shall constitute a quorum. Members shall be appointed for a term of four (4) years or until their respective successors are appointed, except that of the initially appointed Board; two (2) members shall serve for two (2) years, two (2) members for three (3) years, and one (1) member for four (4) years. They shall be residents of the County of Allegheny.

2. One (1) member shall be a physician licensed to practice in the Commonwealth of Pennsylvania; one (1) member shall be an engineer registered by the Commonwealth of Pennsylvania; and three (3) members shall be appointed at large. Compensation for each Appeals Board member shall be determined by the Board of County Commissioners.

3. Meetings of the Appeals Board shall be held at the call of the Chairman and at such other times as the Board may determine. The Appeals Board shall have the power to adopt and enforce such Rules as it may deem necessary to perform its duties as herein provided and may call upon the Air Pollution Control Advisory Committee for technical assistance and advice. All hearings conducted by the Board shall be open to the public and the meetings shall be publicized beforehand. Any person may appear and testify at a hearing, either in person or by duly authorized representative or attorney.

4. The Appeals Board shall conduct hearings where petitions are received for a variance from this Article. Fifty dollars ($50.00) in cash or certified check, payable to the Treasurer of Allegheny County, shall accompany the petition for variance. After a petition is filed with the Appeals Board, the Director may grant a stay of all proceedings pursuant to this Article pending the decision of the Board.

5. All hearings must be conducted in the presence of a quorum, or at least three (3) members of the Appeals Board. The Chairman of the Appeals Board may appoint any member to conduct the hearing and the Chairman or member conducting the hearing shall have authority to administer oaths and do all other necessary and proper duties in the conducting of a hearing.

6. At an Appeals Board hearing the parties involved and the Director may appear with counsel, file written arguments, offer testimony, cross-examine witnesses, or take any combination of such actions.

7. All testimony taken before the Appeals Board shall be under oath and

may be recorded stenographically except that the Appeals Board may require submission of exhibits. The transcripts of the record shall be made available to any person upon payment of the fair charges therefor.

8. Any member conducting the hearing may issue subpoenas for the attendance and testimony of witnesses and the submission of any relevant books and records.

9. The Appeals Board may grant or modify or deny petitions for variance or may revoke a variance already granted. The concurrence of any three (3) members of the Appeals Board shall be necessary for the decision described above.

10. The Appeals Board shall hold a hearing within thirty (30) days after the filing of a petition for a variance and shall make its decision within thirty (30) days after the conclusion of the hearing and shall notify all parties of the record and their counsel of its decision. The Director shall issue appropriate orders requiring compliance with the decision of the Appeals Board. Any decision of the Appeals Board rendered pursuant to this Article shall be final and any appeal therefrom shall be made to the Court of Common Pleas of Allegheny County. Such appeal to the Court of Common Pleas shall be made within thirty (30) days after service of the decision of the Appeals Board. Such appeal to the Court of Common Pleas may be made by any person suffering legal wrong or adversely affected or aggrieved by the decision.

11. Any party or the Director may petition the Appeals Board to modify or cancel variances.

1704. VARIANCES

.1 General

Any person may submit a petition to the Appeals Board for a variance from these Rules and Regulations governing the quality, nature, duration or extent of discharges of air contaminants. The petition shall be filed with the Director who shall act for the Appeals Board in receiving such petition. The petition shall be accompanied by the fee provided in Section 1703.1F.4 and shall include the following information:

A. The name, address and telephone number of the petitioner or other person authorized to receive service of notices.

B. The type of business or activity involved in the application and the street address at which it is conducted.

C. A brief description of the article, machine, equipment or other contrivance or process involved in the application and the emissions occurring therefrom.

D. Each **petition** shall be signed by the petitioner or by some person on his behalf; **where** the person signing is not the petitioner, the petition shall set forth his authority to sign.

E. The section, rule or order from which a variance is sought.

F. The facts showing why compliance with these Rules and Regulations or order cannot be attained.

G. The period of time and the reasons for which the variance is sought.

H. A description of damage or harm that would result to the petitioner from compliance with this Article or order.

I. The requirements that the petitioner can meet and the date when the petitioner can comply with all requirements, including the abatement of emissions that will result.

J. The advantages and disadvantages to the residents of the County that would result from requiring compliance or that would result from granting a variance.

K. A statement of whether any case involving the same equipment or process is pending in any court, civil or criminal.

L. A statement of whether the subject equipment or process is covered by a permit to install and operate issued by the Department and the number of said permit.

M. Such other information and data required by the Board in conformity with the terms, conditions and limitations of these Rules and Regulations.

.2 The Appeals Board may grant such variance if it finds that:

A. The emission occurring or proposed to occur does not constitute a hazard to public health or safety:

and

B. To require compliance with the terms of this Article from which variance is sought would not be in the public interest.

.3 In determining whether a variance should be granted, certain factors shall be taken into consideration by the Appeals Board. These factors shall include but shall not be limited to:

A. Action taken by the applicant to control the emission of air contaminants

B. The efficiency of any control equipment relative to that which would be required to meet the standards set forth in this Article.

C. Any interim control measures.

D. The effect of the emission on ambient air quality.

E. The degree of control relative to similar facilities.

F. The age and degree of obsolescence of the facility in question.

.4 A variance may be granted for a period of time not to exceed one (1) year and under such terms and conditions as shall be specified by the Board. Variance may be renewed by the Appeals Board upon application made at least sixty (60) days prior to the expiration of the term. Renewal application shall be considered in the same manner as the initial petition for variance and the petition for renewal of the variance shall be accompanied by fifty dollars ($50.00) in cash or certified check, payable to the Treasurer of Allegheny County.

.5 A variance may require gradual decrease of emission during the variance period and periodic reports of the improvement program and of compliance with the terms and conditions attached to the variance. Such variance may be revoked or modified for failure to comply with the terms and conditions thereof or for failure to make a periodic report if such is required. Reports on the progress of the program shall be required within such period as may be specified by the Appeals Board.

.6 Nothing in this Section and no variance of renewal granted pursuant hereto shall be construed to prevent or limit the application of the emergency provisions and procedures of this Article.

.7 A petition for variance for an existing facility filed before March 1, 1970, shall operate automatically as a stay of prosecution for violations caused by such facility under the provisions of these Rules and Regulations with respect to which the variance is sought, until July 1, 1970. On and after March 1, 1970, any stay shall be given or withheld according to the provisions of Section 1703.1FA of these Rules and Regulations. Such a stay shall operate to relieve the applicant of compliance with the relevant provisions of Article XIII of the Rules and Regulations of the Allegheny County Health Department which were enacted on the fifth day of July, 1960, and which became effective on the first day of August, 1960.

APPENDIX D

Act No. 222, Session of 1970

An Act amending the act of June 22, 1937 (P.L. 1987), entitled, as amended, "An act to preserve and improve the purity of the waters of the Commonwealth [of Pennsylvania] for the protection of public health, animal and aquatic life, and for industrial consumption, and recreation; empowering and directing the creation of indebtedness or the issuing of non-debt revenue bonds by political subdivisions to provide works to abate pollution; providing protection of water supply; providing for the jurisdiction of courts in the enforcement thereof; requiring the approval of the Attorney General for prosecutions thereunder; providing additional remedies for abating pollution of waters; imposing certain penalties; repealing certain acts; requiring permits for the operation of coal mines, and placing responsibilities upon landowners and land occupiers," defining certain terms and redefining certain other terms, further regulating discharge of sewage and industrial waste and the operation of mines, imposing certain powers and duties on the board, the Department of Health and the

133

Department of Mines and Mineral Industries, adding a member to the board for the purposes of this act, regulating municipal sewage and imposing certain duties on municipalities, further regulating the operation of mines, further providing for certain eminent domain authorization, further stating the responsibilities of landowners and land occupiers, setting forth enforcement procedures and providing penalties. . . .

§ 315. Operation of Mines

(a) No person or municipality shall operate a mine or allow a discharge from a mine into the waters of the Commonwealth unless such operation or discharge is authorized by the rules and regulations of the board or such person or municipality has first obtained a permit from the department. Operation of the mine shall include preparatory work in connection with the opening or reopening of a mine, backfilling, sealing, and other closing procedures, and any other work done on land or water in connection with the mine. A discharge from a mine shall include a discharge which occurs after mining operations have ceased, provided that the mining operations were conducted subsequent to January 1, 1966, under circumstances requiring a permit from the Sanitary Water Board under the provisions of section 315 (b) of this act as it existed under the amendatory act of August 23, 1965 (P.L. 372). The operation of any mine or the allowing of any discharge without a permit or contrary to the terms or conditions of a permit or contrary to the rules and regulations of the board is hereby declared to be a nuisance. Whenever a permit is requested to be issued pursuant to this subsection, and such permit is requested for permission to operate any mining operations, the city, borough, incorporated town or township in which the operation is to be conducted shall be notified by registered mail of the request, at least ten days before the issuance of the permit or before a hearing on the issuance, whichever is first.

(b) The department may require an applicant for a permit to operate a mine, or a permittee holding a permit to operate a mine under the provisions of this section, to post a bond or bonds in favor of the Commonwealth of Pennsylvania and with good and sufficient sureties acceptable to the department to insure that there will be compliance with the law, the rules and regulations of the board, and the provisions and conditions of such permit including conditions pertaining to restoration measures or other provisions insuring that there will be no polluting discharge after mining operations have ceased. The department shall establish the amount of the bond required for each operation and may, from time to time, increase or decrease such amount. Liability under each bond shall continue until such time as the department determines that there is no further significant risk of a pollutional discharge. The failure to post a bond required by the department shall be sufficient cause for withholding the issuance of a permit or for the revocation of an existing permit.

§ 316. Responsibilities of Landowners and Land Occupiers.

Whenever the Sanitary Water Board finds that pollution or a danger of

pollution is resulting from a condition which exists on land in the Commonwealth the board may order the landowner or occupier to correct the condition
in a manner satisfactory to the board or it may order such owner or occupier to
allow a mine operator or other person or agency of the Commonwealth access to
the land to take such action. For the purpose of this section, "landowner"
includes any person holding title to or having a proprietary interest in either
surface or subsurface rights.

For the purpose of collecting or recovering the expense involved in correcting
the condition, the board may assess the amount due in the same manner as civil
penalties are assessed under the provisions of section 605 of this act: Provided,
however, That if the board finds that the condition causing pollution or a danger
of pollution resulted from mining operations conducted prior to January 1,
1966, or, if subsequent to January 1, 1966, under circumstances which did not
require a permit from the Sanitary Water Board under the provisions of
section 315 (b) of this act as it existed under the amendatory act of August 23,
1965 (P.L. 372), then the amount assessed shall be limited to the increase in the
value of the property as a result of the correction of the condition.

If the board finds that the pollution or danger of pollution results from an act
of God in the form of sediment from land for which a complete conservation
plan has been developed by the local soil and water conservation district and the
Soil Conservation Service, U.S.D.A. and the plan has been fully implemented
and maintained, the landowner shall be excluded from the penalties of this
act. . . .

ARTICLE IV. Other Pollutions and Potential Pollution

§ 401. Prohibition Against Other Pollutions

It shall be unlawful for any person or municipality to put or place into any of
the waters of the Commonwealth, or allow or permit to be discharged from
property owned or occupied by such person or municipality into any of the
waters of the Commonwealth, any substance of any kind or character resulting
in pollution as herein defined. Any such discharge is hereby declared to be a
nuisance.

§ 402. Potential Pollution

(a) Whenever the board finds that any activity, not otherwise requiring a
permit under this act, including but not limited to the impounding, handling,
storage, transportation, processing or disposing of materials or substances,
creates a danger of pollution of the waters of the Commonwealth or that
regulation of the activity is necessary to avoid such pollution, the board may, by
rule or regulation, require that such activity be conducted only pursuant to a
permit issued by the department or may otherwise establish the conditions
under which such activity shall be conducted, or the board may issued an order
to a person or municipality regulating a particular activity. Rules and regulations
adopted by the board pursuant to this section shall give the persons or

135

municipalities affected a reasonable period of time to apply for and obtain any permits required by such rules and regulations.

(b) Whenever a permit is required by rules and regulations issued pursuant to this section, it shall be unlawful for a person or municipality to conduct the activity regulated except pursuant to a permit issued by the department. Conducting such activity without a permit, or contrary to the terms or conditions of a permit or conducting an activity contrary to the rules and regulations of the board or conducting an activity contrary to an order issued by the department, is hereby declared to be a nuisance.

APPENDIX E

Code of
Professional Ethics

The reliance of the public and the business community on sound financial reporting and advice on business affairs imposes on the accounting profession an obligation to maintain high standards of technical competence, morality and integrity. To this end, a member or associate of the American Institute of Certified Public Accountants shall at all times maintain independence of thought and action, hold the affairs of his clients in strict confidence, strive continuously to improve his professional skills, observe generally accepted auditing standards, promote sound and informative financial reporting, uphold the dignity and honor of the accounting profession and maintain high standards of personal conduct.

In further recognition of the public interest and his obligation to the profession, a member or associate agrees to comply with the following rules of ethical conduct, the enumeration of which should not be construed as a denial of the existence of other standards of conduct not specifically mentioned:

ARTICLE 1: Relations with Clients and Public

1.01 Neither a member or associate, nor a firm of which he is a partner shall express an opinion on financial statements of any enterprise unless he and his firm are in fact independent with respect to such enterprise.

Independence is not susceptible of precise definition, but is an expression of the professional integrity of the individual. A member or associate, before expressing his opinion on financial statements, has the responsibility of assessing his relationships with an enterprise to determine whether, in the circumstances, he might expect his opinion to be considered independent, objective and unbiased by one who had knowledge of all the facts.

A member or associate will be considered not independent, for example, with respect to any enterprise if he, or one of his partners, (a) during the period of his professional engagement or at the time of expressing his opinion, had, or was committed to acquire, any direct financial interest or material indirect financial interest in the enterprise, or (b) during the period of his professional engagement, at the time of expressing his opinion or during the period covered by the financial statements, was connected with the enterprise as a promoter, underwriter, voting trustee, director, officer or key employee. In cases where a member or associate ceases to be the independent accountant for an enterprise and is subsequently called upon to re-express a previously expressed opinion on financial statements, the phrase "at the time of expressing his opinion" refers only to the time at which the member or associate first expressed his opinion on the financial statements in question. The word "director" is not intended to apply to a connection in such a capacity with a charitable, religious, civic or other similar type of nonprofit organization when the duties performed in such a capacity are such as to make it clear that the member or associate can express an independent opinion on the financial statements. The example cited in this paragraph, of circumstances under which a member or associate will be considered not independent, is not intended to be all-inclusive.

1.02 A member or associate shall not commit an act discreditable to the profession.

1.03 A member or associate shall not violate the confidential relationship between himself and his client.

1.04 Professional service shall not be rendered or offered for a fee which shall be contingent upon the findings or results of such service. This rule does not apply to cases involving Federal, state, or other taxes, in which the findings are those of the tax authorities and not those of the accountant. Fees to be fixed by courts or other public authorities, which are therefore of an indeterminate amount at the time when an engagement is undertaken, are not regarded as contingent fees within the meaning of this rule.

ARTICLE 2: Technical Standards

2.01 A member or associate shall not express his opinion on financial statements unless they have been examined by him, or by a member or employee of his firm, on a basis consistent with the requirements of Rule 2.02.

In obtaining sufficient information to warrant expression of an opinion he may utilize, in part, to the extent appropriate in the circumstances, the reports or other evidence of auditing work performed by another certified public accountant, or firm of public accountants, at least one of whom is a certified public accountant, who is authorized to practice in a state or territory of the United States or the District of Columbia, and whose independence and professional reputation he has ascertained to his satisfaction.

A member or associate may also utilize, in part, to the extent appropriate in the circumstances, the work of public accountants in other countries, but the member or associate so doing must satisfy himself that the person or firm is qualified and independent, that such work is performed in accordance with generally accepted auditing standards, as prevailing in the United States, and that financial statements are prepared in accordance with generally accepted accounting principles, as prevailing in the United States, or are accompanied by the information necessary to bring the statements into accord with such principles.

2.02 In expressing an opinion on representations in financial statements which he has examined, a member or associate may be held guilty of an act discreditable to the profession if:

(a) he fails to disclose a material fact known to him which is not disclosed in the financial statements but disclosure of which is necessary to make the financial statements not misleading; or

(b) he fails to report any material misstatement known to him to appear in the financial statement; or

(c) he is materially negligent in the conduct of his examination or in making his report thereon; or

(d) he fails to acquire sufficient information to warrant expression of an opinion, or his exceptions are sufficiently material to negative the expressions of an opinion; or

(e) he fails to direct attention to any material departure from generally accepted accounting principles or to disclose any material omission of generally accepted auditing procedure applicable in the circumstances. [See Opinion No. 18.]

2.03 A member or associate shall not permit his name to be associated with these statements purporting to show financial position or results of operations in such a manner as to imply that he is acting as an independent public accountant unless he shall:

(a) express an unqualified opinion; or

(b) express a qualified opinion; or

(c) express an adverse opinion; or

(d) disclaim an opinion on the statements taken as a whole and indicate clearly his reasons therefor; or

(e) when unaudited financial statements are presented on his stationery without his comments, disclose prominently on each page of the financial statements that they were not audited. [See Opinions No. 8, 13 and 15.]

2.04 A member or associate shall not permit his name to be used in conjunction with any forecast of the results of future transactions in a manner which may lead to the belief that the member or associate vouches for the accuracy of the forecast.

ARTICLE 3: Promotional Practices

3.01 A member or associate shall not advertise his professional attainments or services.

Publication in a newspaper, magazine or similar medium of an announcement or what is technically known as a card is prohibited.

A listing in a directory is restricted to the name, title, address and telephone number of the person or firm, and it shall not appear in a box, or other form of display or in a type or style which differentiates it from other listings in the same directory. Listing of the same name in more than one place in a classified directory is prohibited.

3.02 A member or associate shall not endeavor, directly or indirectly, to obtain clients by solicitation. [See Opinion No. 18.]

3.03 A member or associate shall not make a competitive bid for a professional engagement. Competitive bidding for public accounting services is not in the public interest, is a form of solicitation, and is unprofessional.*

3.04 Commissions, brokerage, or other participation in the fees or profits of professional work shall not be allowed or paid directly or indirectly by a member or associate to any individual or firm not regularly engaged or employed in the practice of public accounting as a principal occupation.

Commissions, brokerage, or other participation in the fees, charges or profits of work recommended or turned over to any individual or firm not regularly engaged or employed in the practice of public accounting as a principal occupation, as incident to services for clients, shall not be accepted directly, or indirectly by a member or associate.

ARTICLE 4: Operating Practices

4.01 A firm or partnership, all the individual members of which are members of the Institute, may describe itself as "Members of the American Institute of Certified Public Accountants," but a firm or partnership, not all the individual members of which are members of the Institute, or an individual practicing under a style denoting a partnership when in fact there be no partner or partners, or a corporation, or an individual or individuals practicing under a style

*On the advice of legal counsel that Rule 3.03 subjects the Institute and its representatives to risks under the Federal antitrust laws, the Institute's executive committee, Council and committee on professional ethics have decided that the Institute will continue to refrain from taking any disciplinary action against any member or associate under Rule 3.03 until there has been a change in circumstances that would justify a different opinion on the legal status of the Rule.

denoting a corporate organization shall not use the designation "Members of the American Institute of Certified Public Accountants."

4.02   A member or associate shall not practice in the name of another unless he is in partnership with him or in his employ, nor shall he allow any person to practice in his name who is not in partnership with him or in his employ.

This rule shall not prevent a partnership or its successors from continuing to practice under a firm name which consists of or includes the name or names of one or more former partners, nor shall it prevent the continuation of a partnership name for a reasonable period of time by the remaining partner practicing as a sole proprietor after the withdrawal or death of one or more partners.

4.03   A member or associate in his practice of public accounting shall not permit an employee to perform for the member's or associate's clients any services which the member or associate himself or his firm is not permitted to perform.

4.04   A member or associate shall not engage in any business or occupation conjointly with that of a public accountant, which is incompatible or inconsistent therewith.

4.05   A member or associate engaged in an occupation in which he renders services of a type performed by public accountants, or renders other professional services, must observe the by-laws and Code of Professional Ethics of the Institute in the conduct of that occupation.

4.06   A member or associate shall not be an officer, director, stockholder, representative, or agent of any corporation engaged in the practice of public accounting in any state or territory of the United States or the District of Columbia.

ARTICLE 5: Relations with Fellow Members

5.01   A member or associate shall not encroach upon the practice of another public accountant. A member or associate may furnish service to those who request it.

5.02   A member or associate who receives an engagement for services by referral from another member or associate shall not discuss or accept an extension of his services beyond the specific engagement without first consulting with the referring member or associate.

5.03   Direct or indirect offer of employment shall not be made by a member or associate to an employee of another public accountant without first informing such accountant. This rule shall not be construed so as to inhibit negotiations with anyone who of his own initiative or in response to public advertisement shall apply to a member or associate for employment.

*   *   *

OPINION NO. 18: Fees and Professional Standards

Offering to perform services for an inadequate fee may be evidence of solicitation.

In determining the amount of his fee, a CPA may assess the degree of responsibility being assumed in the engagement, the time and manpower required to perform the service in conformity with the standards of the profession, the skills needed to discharge his professional obligation to the client and the public, the value to the client of the services rendered, and the customary charges of professional colleagues. Other considerations may also be involved. No single factor can be controlling.

It is characteristic of all professional persons to be more concerned with fulfilling their responsibilities to the public than with immediate financial reward. On occasions they may appropriately choose to serve a client for a fee less than cost, or indeed without any compensation whatever.

However, to quote a fee in advance of an engagement in an amount clearly inadequate to provide fair compensation for performing service in accordance with accepted professional standards may be regarded, in some circumstances, as evidence of solicitation in violation of Rule 3.02 of the Code of Professional Ethics. Without attempting to specify all circumstances that might be relevant in determining the propriety of a particular quotation, it would be appropriate to consider whether there were any facts suggesting that such an inadequate fee had been fixed as a part of a plan or design to solicit business.

In such cases of inadequate fees there may be a temptation to minimize losses by reducing the amount of work below that required by Rule 2.02 of the Code, with serious consequences for third parties who rely upon opinions of financial statements.

APPENDIX F

International Business Machines Corporation   Armonk, New York 10504
914/765-1900

NOVEMBER 20, 1970

ATTENTION: MARKETING MANAGER

422814

GENTLEMEN:

WE ARE AGAIN REMINDING YOU OF IBM'S POLICY ON GIFTS. NO IBM EMPLOYEE OR MEMBER OF HIS FAMILY MAY ACCEPT GIFTS, SERVICES, DISCOUNTS, OR FAVORS FROM THOSE WITH WHOM WE DO BUSINESS, OR CONSIDER DOING BUSINESS. EMPLOYEES WHO VIOLATE THIS POLICY ARE SUBJECT TO DISCIPLINARY ACTION.

WE ALSO ASK THAT DONATIONS TO CHARITY NOT BE MADE IN THE NAME OF IBM OR ITS EMPLOYEES.

I FEEL SURE YOU UNDERSTAND THE REASONS FOR THIS POLICY AND WILL COOPERATE WITH OUR EFFORTS TO MAKE SURE THAT IBM DECISIONS ON THE SELECTION OF SUPPLIERS ARE MADE WITHOUT ANY POSSIBLE REFERENCE TO PERSONAL RELATIONSHIPS.

IBM APPRECIATES THE ASSISTANCE OUR SUPPLIERS HAVE GIVEN US THROUGH THE YEARS, AND WE LOOK FORWARD TO CONTINUED CORDIAL RELATIONSHIPS.

SINCERELY YOURS,

INDEX

A

Accountants, **70***
Administrations, *25*
Advertising, 67,92,93,95
Agriculture, U.S. Dept. of, *35*
AICPA, 70
Air Pollution Control Administration, *34*
American Management Assoc., *3*
American Revolution, *18*
Anthropology, *15*
Anti-trust legislation, *29*
Aquinas, *3,31*
Aristotle, *16*
Attitude, *16*
Automation, 48

*Bold type is case material

B

Bargaining, 84
Barnard, *6*
Batchelder, *27*
Behavior, *14,15*
Bentham, *18,87*
Berle, *28*
Bias, 58
Bill of Rights, *27*
Blacks, *24,26,27,54,***58,59,105**
"Blockbusting," 111
Board of Directors, 68
Boulware, Lemuel, 82
"Boulwarism," 82
Boycotts, *3*